CHANEL

ILLUSTRATED

LANNOO

CONTENTS

6	ANNA BLACHUT	132	KELLY SMITH
18	AURORE DE LA MORINERIE	142	LENA KER
30	BLAIR BREITENSTEIN	148	LYDIA BOURHILL
40	CECILIA CARLSTEDT	154	MILA GISLON
50	CHLOE TAKAHASHI	166	MIYUKI OHASHI
60	ELIZABETH LAMB SZÉKELY	178	NICOLE JARECZ
72	ÉLODIE CLAVIER	188	NINA COSFORD
80	GLADYS PERINT PALMER	202	POSUKA DEMIZU
92	HWI	212	SHAY BEN IZHACK
102	JENNY CHUI	220	STEVE QUILES
110	JOANNA LAYLA	232	TANYA CHULKOVA
122	KAROLINA PAWELCZYK	240	VIOLA LI

ANNA BLACHUT

CHANEL

ILLUSTRATED

Anna Blachut was just 14 years old when her first fashion illustration was published in a book. Her natural talent for drawing emerged from a young age, when her parents would often find her doodling in the margins of books and on restaurant napkins. They encouraged her to express herself creatively as well as academically.

When she went off to university, Blachut immersed herself in different cultures. The Swiss talent, who hails from Geneva, studied illustration at the University of Edinburgh and at Parsons School of Design in Paris. These experiences introduced her to a rich world of creative exchanges – with peers, industry experts and mentors like the renowned woodblock printer and illustrator Jonathan Gibbs, whom she considers a true guide in her artistic development.

For Blachut, her training was an opportunity to take a deep dive into different ways of seeing and communicating as an artist. She grasped it with enthusiasm, refining her creative vision along the way. During those years, she honed her craft by starting to illustrate for magazines, private clients and hotels across Europe and America, cultivating connections with like-minded creative people and brands.

Blachut's far-ranging frame of reference is reflected in her body of work, which makes use of coloured pencils, Indian ink and watercolours to create fashion illustrations and still-life drawings that possess a dream-like quality. With artistic inspirations like Gustav Klimt, Paul Cézanne, Erté, Salvador Dalí and Joan Miró, it's no wonder the Art Nouveau and Art Deco eras reverberate in Blachut's aesthetic, which foregrounds colour as a defining characteristic.

The world of fashion was never far off. In the early 2000s, Blachut loved to leaf through fashion magazines, admiring Chanel campaigns and pinning them to her bedroom wall. Their black and white simplicity fascinated her, a feeling heightened by the first time she set foot in a Chanel boutique in Geneva. Blachut felt a sense of wonder there. The cream and black interior and the incredible kindness with which the Chanel team greeted her left an indelible mark. Her first collaboration with the brand was unique and cutting-edge. Chanel asked her to create a limited-edition animated artwork that was to be minted as a digital collectible NFT. She created it especially for an exclusive gathering of the maison's top executives in Arles, taking inspiration from Chanel's iconic house codes such as the camellia and the Boy bag – but transformed, in typical Chanel fashion, into an expression of the current zeitgeist.

Ultimately, it's all of these elements – colour, mood, music, art, places, people and the narrative behind it all – that make Blachut tick. It's not just the fashion show; it's also what goes on behind the scenes, the things that are shown and the things that are hidden. Through her art, Blachut intends to capture more than just a fashion look or a branded image; she's setting out to illustrate a moment in time, the essence of a brand's vision and the unique story it tells.

THE FIRST TIME BLACHUT SET FOOT IN A CHANEL BOUTIQUE IN GENEVA, SHE FELT A SENSE OF WONDER

*The artist's fashion illustrations and still-life
drawings possess a dream-like quality*

Blachut's training was an opportunity to take a deep dive into different ways of seeing and communicating as an artist

Through her art, Anna Blachut is setting out to illustrate a moment in time, the essence of a brand's vision and the unique story it tells

The first time Blachut set foot in a Chanel boutique in Geneva, she felt a sense of wonder

AURORE DE LA MORINERIE

N°5
CHANEL
PARIS

EAU DE PARFUM

In the span of a few decades, French illustrator Aurore de la Morinerie has built a meditative body of work that encapsulates her never-ending and always-enriching search for simplicity and abstraction.

In childhood, she developed an awareness that drawing allowed her to observe and analyse the world. Drawn to the history of Western painting, Aurore de la Morinerie was captivated by the possibilities of artistic expression – how gesture and movement can leave a tangible trace on the surface that communicates a vision.

Her family – she hails from Normandy, France – encouraged her talent and decision to pursue drawing as a profession. Initially, however, she chose to train as a fashion designer at the Duperré School of Applied Arts, deepening her knowledge of fashion and draftsmanship. Her strong interest in the East Asian arts led her to also study Chinese calligraphy. The practice helped her to cultivate her love for ink, paper, water and brushwork. Embracing both cultural traditions allowed Aurore de la Morinerie to fuse the two in her fledgling illustration practice.

She set out on her own soon after her studies, feeling a desire to work independently. In the early 1990s, Aurore de la Morinerie earned recognition as an artist of rare evocative talent in the fashion world for her work with an impressive roster of luxury houses. Her drawings, often of single objects, convey the spirit of her subject matter in an artful, gestural and stylised manner. With Chanel, the journey began by creating illustrations for women's magazines centred on perfume and the brand's iconic, angular perfume bottles, which stood out to the artist for their simplicity and elegance.

Even as a student, the artist was inspired by the influence Gabrielle 'Coco' Chanel had on fashion, the sartorial revolution the legendary designer brought to women's clothing, and the power of aesthetics at large. The timeless elegance of Chanel silhouettes paired so perfectly with the black and natural tones of the garments had a significant impact and resonated strongly with her artistic approach. From the perfume to the jewellery and the relentless attention to detail in each of Chanel's product lines, the overall image that Chanel projects has been an influence on her plastic language, remaining a natural source of inspiration for the French illustrator.

In her wide-ranging work, Aurore de la Morinerie also explores nature themes, landscapes, animals, plants and design, making use of brushwork balancing between lightness and calligraphic strength. Photography has long accompanied and enriched her artistic practice, which is evident in the sometimes ephemeral or instantaneous nature of her drawings.

CHANEL'S ICONIC, ANGULAR PERFUME BOTTLES STOOD OUT TO AURORE DE LA MORINERIE FOR THEIR SIMPLICITY AND ELEGANCE

PARIS - VENISE

CHANEL

PARIS

*The overall image that Chanel projects has been
an influence on the artist's visual language*

A strong interest in the East Asian arts led
Aurore de la Morinerie to also study Chinese calligraphy

The artist's drawings convey the spirit of her subject matter in an artful, gestural and stylised manner

The artist makes use of brushwork balancing
between lightness and calligraphic strength

BLAIR
BREITENSTEIN

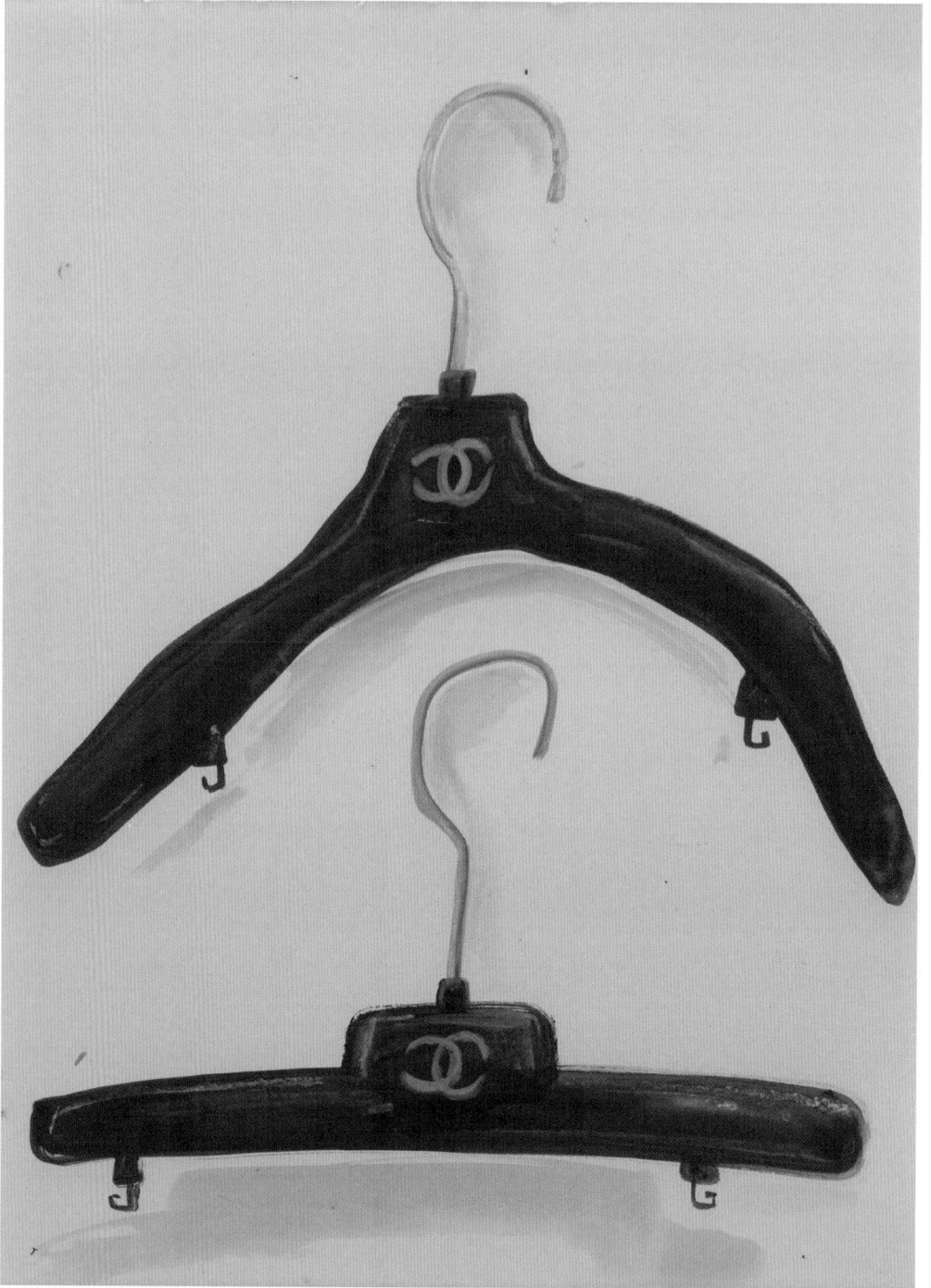

The fashion illustrations of Blair Breitenstein invite many modifiers of magnitude. She captures high fashion through bold lines, intensely layered watercolours, exaggerated proportions, big eyes, big lips and big hairstyles. Rather than simply depicting what her subjects are wearing, the American illustrator's aesthetic can be described as expressionist: it conveys the emotional impact of fashion more than realistically reflecting it, and uses illustration as a tool to evoke those emotions in the viewer.

As a young girl, Breitenstein was introduced to both the creative process and fashion as part of her upbringing. Her grandfather was an artist and animator for Walt Disney, and she grew up watching him paint. Doodling next to him felt natural and she picked up a love for creating – drawing and painting – by osmosis. Breitenstein took art classes in school, and studied fine art in college, but has always taken an instinctive approach to creating: sketching freely, exploring media at home, and more generally evolving and developing her style outside the classroom.

Breitenstein's obsession with fashion magazines was influenced by her grandmother, who subscribed to all the big titles like *Vogue*, *Harper's Bazaar* and *W*. The dream-like world of editorials, especially the more theatrical ones, spoke to her. In those settings, Chanel silhouettes were always some of her favourites to draw. She remembers vividly feeling compelled to sketch the French house's Spring-Summer 2014 Ready-to-Wear and Fall-Winter 2014/15 Ready-to-Wear collections when she saw them online. Whimsical and theatrical from the hair and make-up to the set designs – a Chanel contemporary art gallery and a Chanel supermarket, respectively – the shows mesmerised the fledgling illustrator. When Breitenstein took her artwork to Tumblr, then Instagram, and later contributed illustrations to *Harper's Bazaar Mexico* in 2014, her confidence to pursue art professionally grew.

Breitenstein continued to draw Chanel looks on her own, purely as personal passion projects. She loves playing with the house's many iconic textures and emblems – like tweed, camellias, pearls and quilting – that give the brand its strong identity. Those works attracted the brand's attention and led to the house inviting Breitenstein to collaborate. Over the years, the illustrator has created artwork for Chanel events in New York City and collaborated with many other high fashion brands, like Prada and Alaïa.

Influenced by high fashion photography as well as other fashion illustrators like René Gruau, Ruben Toledo and David Downton, Breitenstein similarly harnesses colour, texture and gesture in her work, capturing glamour and movement with a spontaneous boldness. She doesn't do preliminary sketching, preferring to dive right in, letting the materials lead her in a mix of pastels, watercolour and acrylic paint. The results draw the viewer into a playful, abstract and chic world of fashion. Yet, no piece, whether in a small or large sketchbook, is ever too precious for Breitenstein. That irreverent attitude is reminiscent of Gabrielle Chanel's finest moments horse riding in women's trousers or throwing unfussy parties in her French Riviera house – Coco, too, kept it fun.

BREITENSTEIN LOVES PLAYING WITH CHANEL'S MANY ICONIC TEXTURES AND EMBLEMS THAT GIVE THE BRAND ITS STRONG IDENTITY

Breitenstein captures high fashion through bold lines, intensely layered watercolours, exaggerated proportions, big eyes, big lips and big hairstyles

The illustrator loves playing with the house's many iconic textures and emblems –
like tweed, camellias, pearls and quilting – that give the brand its strong identity

Breitenstein harnesses colour, texture and gesture in her work, capturing glamour and movement with a spontaneous boldness

CECILIA CARLSTEDT

CHANEL

ILLUSTRATED

The flat surface and its possibilities have always held a special appeal for Cecilia Carlstedt. With a mother who illustrated children's books, drawing came naturally and was very much encouraged. The creative field beckoned.

At secondary school in her hometown of Stockholm, Carlstedt chose to study art and even landed her first small editorial fashion illustration gigs for Swedish *Elle* and *Damernas Värld*, one of Sweden's oldest women's magazines. This was the 1990s – at the peak of glossy magazines' power – when photography and graphic expression produced a wealth of visual treasures. The experiences sparked Carlstedt's interest in fashion illustration and launched her freelance career. But with doubts about the profession's viability, she instead considered going into graphic design.

Carlstedt studied art history at the University of Stockholm, immersing herself in the theoretical aspects of the fine arts and their evolution across time and cultures. But she missed the hands-on process of creating. So, she left Stockholm and moved to London to study graphic design at the London College of Communication with a focus on experimental image-making. The programme opened up a world of different experiences: she spent a semester at the Fashion Institute of Technology, or FIT, in New York and cut her teeth at various graphic design studios.

Over time, the bond Carlstedt had started to forge with the world of fashion strengthened. At first, old *Vogue* covers and the legendary illustrations of René Gruau and Georges Lepape lifted the veil of expressive art for Carlstedt. Today, the full-time illustrator pulls from the work of her heroes across many creative fields. She finds herself returning to the work of early modernists like Picasso, Matisse and Sonia Delaunay. And she takes inspiration from the work of contemporary painters, like Elizabeth Peyton, Marlene Dumas and fellow Swede Mamma Andersson. What connects these inspirations is their bold approach to contrasting, evocative colour and vivid graphic lines. Those features figure prominently in Carlstedt's work, too – enriched with loose brush strokes and faint pen marks, or even bits of collage, elements uniquely combined to add tension and depth.

The results are visually striking, feminine and personal images that capture emotions, atmospheres and moods. In other work, Carlstedt homes in on a more stripped-back aesthetic, using clean lines paired with solid colour fields to delineate a figure and convey a particular brand image. This is where the illustrator's love of Chanel comes into the picture. Once more, something two-dimensional attracts the Swedish illustrator the most: the French fashion house's iconic monogram with the interlocking Cs. A prime example of a perfect symbol – suggestive, expressive and meaningful, executed with just a few clean, graphic curved lines – Carlstedt loves to illustrate Chanel pieces that figure the monogram prominently. And, based as it is on Gabrielle 'Coco' Chanel's world-famous affectionate moniker, the monogram also happens to contain the illustrator's own initials – a further boon that makes the recognisable monogram especially resonant to her.

CARLSTEDT LOVES TO ILLUSTRATE CHANEL PIECES THAT FIGURE THE ICONIC MONOGRAM WITH THE INTERLOCKING C'S PROMINENTLY

The illustrator takes inspiration from the work of contemporary painters, like Elizabeth Peyton, Marlene Dumas and fellow Swede Mamma Andersson

The results are visually striking, feminine and personal images that capture emotions, atmospheres and moods

CHLOE TAKAHASHI

CHANEL

ILLUSTRATED

classicflap

Slingback

CHANEL

Chloe Takahashi

CHANEL
PARIS

Chloe Takahashi

Chloe Takahashi's creative path has been anything but linear. A former finance professional, she spent years in the world of investment banking and real estate in Tokyo and New York before recognising the quiet pull of something vital that was missing. That sense – subtle at first – gradually led her back to fashion and drawing, two passions rooted deep in her childhood in Japan.

In primary school, she took part in weekly 'croquis days', where students made sketches and displayed their youthful work in the corridor. Even then, Takahashi's talent stood out. She once dreamt of becoming a manga artist, but her artistic pursuits faded as academic and professional demands took over. Years later, as she reconsidered her life's direction, illustration returned to her in a very natural way.

The Japanese illustrator began spontaneously sketching fashion imagery, turning to Instagram as a kind of creative diary and posting street-style drawings day after day. Her account grew quickly – it's now at 49,600 and counting – and as a result of the positive feedback and energy, she started to feel like herself again. What began as a little side project soon revealed itself as a major calling. She decided it was time to finally return to doing what she loved.

Takahashi's style is shaped by her lifelong admiration for Japanese manga artists, vintage American comic books and high fashion. Her illustrations are playful yet composed, full of personality and poise. There is often a thread of nostalgia woven through her compositions – an element of *mujo*, the Japanese aesthetic principle that finds beauty in impermanence. Her figures often channel that ethos, evoking a classic charm while also appearing busily in action, always on the move. Takahashi captures gesture and expression with ease, bringing emotion to the surface through colour, styling and pose.

Unsurprisingly, Takahashi returns often to themes of female strength, individuality and timeless style – motifs that naturally align with the legacy of Gabrielle Chanel. Her illustrated women are confident and strong, sometimes with a knowing glance or subtle attitude. In them, we find the spirit of independence and elegance. Takahashi's admiration for Chanel's classic, androgynous aesthetic finds form in the fine detailing she so often highlights – pearls, brooches, pocket trims – elements that give her characters both polish and personality.

Her fashion drawings of Chanel reflect the brand's duality: strength and softness, structure and flair. The bold black lines Takahashi favours echo the dramatic contrasts used by both the house of Chanel and the illustrator she cites as an inspiration: Miyuki Morimoto. In this visual conversation, Takahashi finds a place of her own.

At the centre of it all is Takahashi's deep love for drawing – something that has never left her. With each stroke, she merges her artistic style with broader traditions of fashion, culture and art. And like the story of Gabrielle Chanel, a fearless independent woman, her journey is one of strength and self-determination – returning her to the joy of creation.

TAKAHASHI'S PREFERRED THEMES OF FEMALE STRENGTH, INDIVIDUALITY AND TIMELESS STYLE ALIGN WITH THE LEGACY OF GABRIELLE CHANEL

CHANEL

CHANEL

Chloe Takahashi

Takahashi's style is shaped by her lifelong admiration for Japanese manga artists, vintage American comic books and high fashion

A GIRL SHOULD BE TWO THINGS: CLASSY AND FABULOUS

RRRING!

Chloe Takahashi

"To remain irreplaceable
We must always
be different." *

*Quote by Gabrielle Chanel

CHANEL

CHANEL

Chloe Takahashi

Chanel Beauty.

Chloe Takahashi

Takahashi's illustrations are playful yet composed, full of personality and poise

Shopping in Paris

Chloe Takahachi

The illustrator's preferred themes of female strength, individuality and timeless style align with the legacy of Gabrielle Chanel

"A woman who uses no perfume has no future." *

*Quote by Gabrielle Chanel

ELIZABETH LAMB SZÉKELY

In Elizabeth Lamb Székely's drawings, there's a common thread from fairy tales to fashion. The Australian illustrator creates art that is whimsical and striking in equal measure, often using her vivid imagination to tell a story – from a Gothic-tinged lady in mourning to a parade of 1920s flapper girls that embody a 'Gatsby-meets-Chanel' aesthetic.

Székely's love of drawing was encouraged by her school art teachers. At their prompting, she pursued a bachelor's degree in fashion design and merchandising at the Royal Melbourne Institute of Technology, or RMIT. As she developed her skills there in a focused, dedicated way, she started to realise that illustration could be a viable career path. When she took her first real steps as a professional, she marvelled at her ability to actually sell her work – and get paid for doing what she loved most.

At first, Székely worked as a technical illustrator for clothing production, but over time, fashion illustration – as an artistic pursuit – came to the foreground. Freelance opportunities grew, and when Székely was offered the opportunity to create her first book cover, she felt the full excitement of seeing her illustration work on display in shops. That moment was pivotal in her conviction that this artistic path was the direction she wanted to follow.

The journey led to a body of work that's in constant evolution. Székely relishes this process, sometimes revisiting ideas and techniques that she has previously explored, and at other times growing into new, unfamiliar modes that keep her creativity fresh and exciting. When looking for inspiration, René Gruau is forever top of mind for her, but the work of fashion designers who excelled at illustration continues to influence her as well, like the sketches of legendary couturiers Christian Dior, Yves Saint Laurent and Christian Lacroix. Considering the thread of Gothic elements in her work, it's no surprise that Tim Burton figures, too. And in a sense,

Gabrielle Chanel, with her great love of black, fits that mood perfectly.

The French fashion house of Chanel already attracted Székely's attention when she was younger and working part-time at an Australian department store's perfume counter. Experiencing Chanel's beauty and perfume lines in their sleek packaging introduced her to the brand's consistency of vision. Gabrielle Chanel's legacy as an innovative businesswoman included a prescient understanding of accessibility – epitomised by the transformative power of lipstick – which helped cement the brand's enduring success.

The simple but effective magnetism that a well-chosen stroke of colour can achieve permeates Székely's work. When using her favourite media of pencil to paper, sometimes with watercolour paints, paper collage and digital work mixed in, she maintains a sense of lightness. Whether juxtaposing cream and black in a silhouette featuring Chanel's iconic two-tone shoe, adding pops of fuchsia pink or the glimmer of a classic set of pearls, Székely evokes a feminine vision of strong sophistication in her drawings. Like Chanel, that will never go out of style.

CHANEL ALREADY ATTRACTED SZÉKELY'S ATTENTION WHEN SHE WAS WORKING PART-TIME AT AN AUSTRALIAN DEPARTMENT STORE'S PERFUME COUNTER

The Australian illustrator creates art that is whimsical and striking in equal measure

*Székely evokes a feminine vision of
strong sophistication in her drawings*

Experiencing Chanel's beauty and perfume lines in their sleek packaging introduced Székely to the brand's consistency of vision

ÉLODIE CLAVIER

CHANEL
ILLUSTRATED

LEVERNIS
NAIL COLOUR

617
HOLIDAY

CHANEL

Even as a child, Élodie Clavier fantasised about making a living with her art. She filled scraps of paper with silhouettes and took drawing classes, always occupied with creating. In art school in Nantes, a teacher first pointed out what would become her signature style – a distinctive, exaggerated line. Slowly but surely, she began to pave the way for illustration to turn into more than just a hobby – it became an ambition.

With her training as a foundation, Clavier continued developing her technique and style largely on her own, sketching from home, refining her eye and hand. A pivotal point came when she met her agent and began working professionally as an artist.

Chanel became one of her earliest collaborators – no small feat in the pre-Instagram days. At the time, the French house was searching for an illustrator and spotted a sketch of a simple black and white Chanel shopping bag on Clavier's website, executed in the illustrator's characteristic spontaneously stylised manner, using ink. Chanel invited Clavier to live-draw at a Place Vendôme event in Paris, marking a significant milestone – and the beginning of a fruitful creative collaboration that is still going strong today.

One of Clavier's most drawn subjects is the Chanel camellia, a lasting house emblem. In her work for Chanel, Clavier distils the spirit of the brand into a few essential strokes – capturing silhouettes with elongated limbs, in the middle of making elegant gestures and experiencing chic moments. Clavier's refined yet bold and decisive touch works perfectly as a tool to capture this world of luxury and beautiful clothes. Dreamy places of leisure figure in her work regularly too, creating a picture-perfect classicist backdrop to her scenes. They are distinctly French, ranging from Paris' Haussmannian boulevards to the country houses of the Provence, enveloped in lush lavender gardens.

Clavier's artistic influences span eras and disciplines yet are unified by elegance and precision. She draws inspiration from the fashion sketches of iconic designers and from influential illustrators like Jean-Philippe Delhomme and Sempé. These references inform the expressive visual language punctuated by fluid ink lines and restrained detail that Clavier has made her own, whether drawn by hand or on a graphic tablet.

Today, Clavier continues to work on a wide range of projects across fashion and luxury, from whimsical packaging designs to exclusive event invitations for luxury hospitality brands as well as imagery for beauty brands. She brings not only a visual elegance to her illustrations but also an emotional resonance, creating pieces that feel both personal and timeless. Clavier's ultimate goal with her work is as much about depicting atmosphere as it is about rendering form – capturing not just how something looks, but also how it feels.

CHANEL BECAME ONE OF CLAVIER'S EARLIEST COLLABORATORS – NO SMALL FEAT IN THE PRE-INSTAGRAM DAYS

*Clavier's refined yet bold and decisive touch works perfectly
as a tool to capture this world of luxury and beautiful clothes*

*Clavier distils the spirit of the brand
into a few essential strokes*

GLADYS
PERINT
PALMER

CHANEL

ILLUSTRATED

Gladys Perint Palmer was able to observe fashion and drawing up close from the age of two, while perched on her dress designer mother's lap. It didn't take long for the young Palmer to start drawing, too. Growing up in Budapest, she took to the page as often as she could. And though she did get in trouble doodling in her exercise books, it also brought her positive attention. She was told that her drawings were unusually developed for her age, and that her powers of observation were remarkable.

Going to art school was a natural progression – first to Central Saint Martins in London, then to Parsons in New York. 'Learn the rules, then break them' is just one lesson instilled in Palmer by Muriel Pemberton, the fashion designer, painter and teacher who taught at CSM. Another inspiring mentor was Elizabeth Suter, a fashion illustrator and journalist whose fast and confident style left a tangible trace on Palmer's own dynamic signature line work.

Continuous, bold and decisively sparse, the lines that make up Palmer's figure drawings encapsulate silhouettes in motion, often seen from the side or the back. In this oblique way, the illustrator masterfully captures a personality, brand aesthetic and fashion style. Through the prism of the designer's model, Palmer pays close attention to pose, proportion, and the particularities of an industry she has been steeped in for close to seven decades.

While a student at Parsons in the sixties, Palmer received her first professional commission, nine pages in American *Harper's Bazaar*. She was called upon to produce a *Vogue* cover the same year. As a result of her tenure as a fashion editor and columnist – first at the *South China Morning Post*, then at the *San Francisco Examiner* – she entered the orbit of many fashion designers, including Karl Lagerfeld. He always used to call her Madame Palmer, while she called him Monsieur Lagerfeld, a sign of mutual respect between two prolific creative powerhouses.

Over the years, Palmer has illustrated dozens of Chanel designs, which have appeared mostly in international magazines. Each drawing follows the evolution of the French house – through the eras, each inventive iteration of the Chanel look is adapted to the times, and each distinctive feature captures the spirit and mood of the theme Lagerfeld looked to convey. From the attitude and bold make-up of a 1990s Linda Evangelista atop a motorcycle, to the intimate rapport of Lagerfeld conversing with Ines de la Fressange, and the aloofness of a haute-couture turn on the catwalk, Palmer brings out the awe the fashion world stirs in us all.

Today, Palmer lives in San Rafael, California and is Executive Director of Fashion at San Francisco's Academy of Art. With students of her own to mentor now, she's eager to transmit her love and enthusiasm of living a life led by art, ambition and talent. She urges them: 'Just draw, draw, draw, never stop, if you wish to make it your career.'

AS A RESULT OF HER TENURE AS A FASHION EDITOR AND COLUMNIST, PALMER ENTERED THE ORBIT OF MANY FASHION DESIGNERS, INCLUDING KARL LAGERFELD

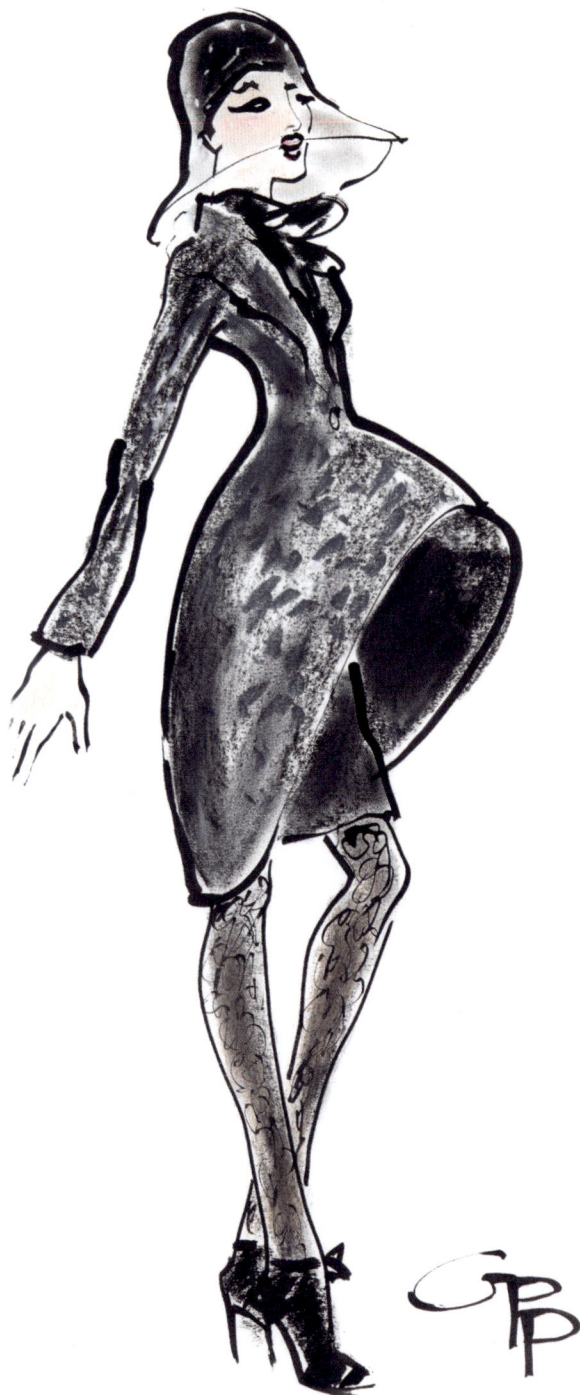

*Continuous, bold and decisively sparse, the lines that make up
Palmer's figure drawings encapsulate silhouettes in motion*

*Palmer pays close attention to pose, proportion, and the particularities of
an industry she has been steeped in for close to seven decades*

Chanel
Teacup hat, pearl buttons-cum-necklace,
seamed stockings

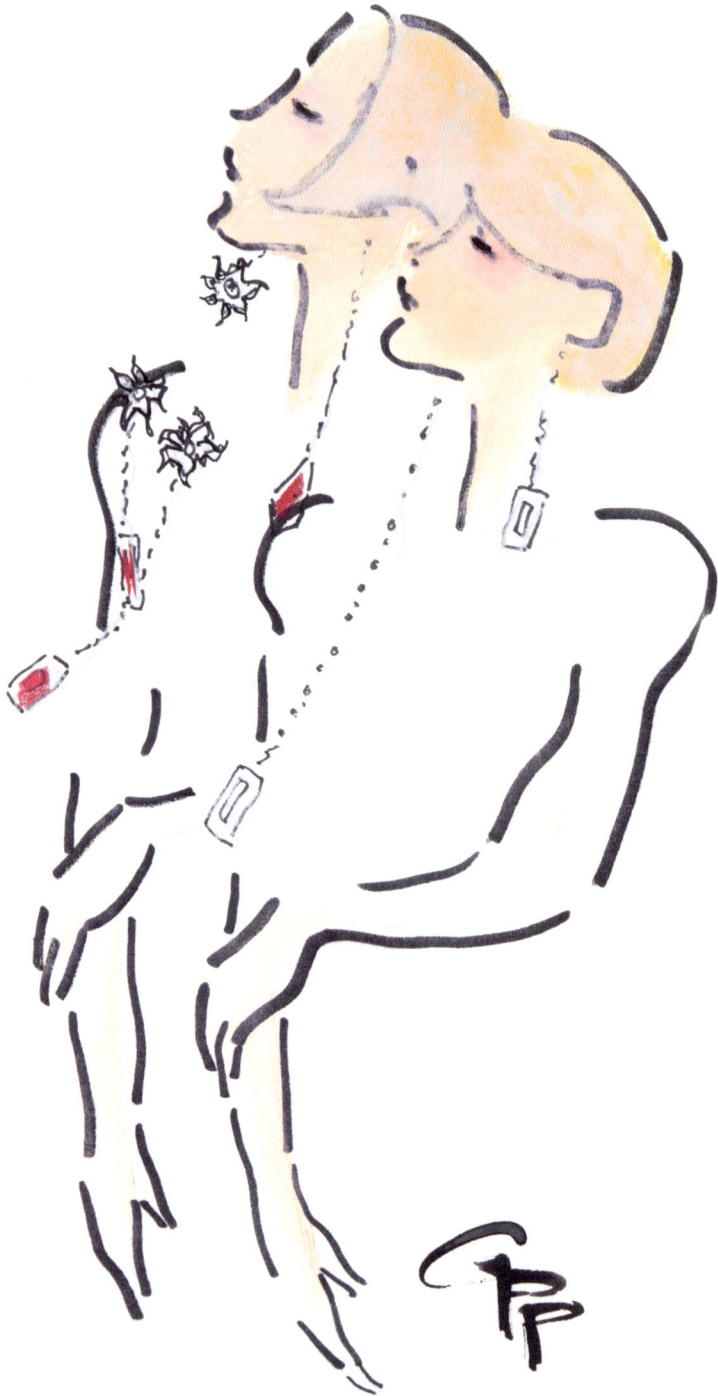

CHANEL HAUTE COUTURE

GPP

The illustrator brings out the awe
the fashion world stirs in us all

HWI

CHANEL
ILLUSTRATED

Sometimes a person's artistic side can lay dormant for a while, before springing back up when the time is right. For See Hwi Yeoh, that part of herself – whether expressed through singing, dancing or doodling as a child – blossomed into a more significant one when she went to college. There, the Malaysian-born illustrator, who went to Iowa State University to pursue a bachelor's degree in psychology, got her first tablet. The digital tool spurred Yeoh to take up her sketching practice again and led her to realise how much she loved fashion illustration.

During the Covid pandemic, much like everybody else, Yeoh started spending more time at home. For fun, she created an Instagram account to share her art with the world. Organically, brands started to tap her talents for live illustration gigs at openings or events. It didn't take long for Yeoh to decide to become a full-time artist. The live buzz of the events that gave the illustrator her start still means a lot to her – she still relishes in capturing the energy of a moment in real time through her drawings.

Though fully self-taught, Yeoh has taken online courses over the years – including a painting course by one of her biggest inspirations, Kerrie Hess. In her own work, she likes to incorporate elements like textures, colours and even swatches from make-up into an illustration, as a tactile way to explore the dynamic relationship between fashion and storytelling.

The house of Chanel found its way onto Yeoh's radar when she was 15 years old. In autumn 2011, Karl Lagerfeld introduced the brand's iconic Boy bag, a boxy, pared-back design that's slightly less feminine than other Chanel handbags. A reference to Gabrielle Chanel's own tomboyish style and the nickname for her longtime lover Arthur 'Boy' Capel, it's an example of Lagerfeld's visionary capacity to create novelty out of the brand and its founder's storied pasts. The design's strong lines, though still glamorous, evoke the angular, elegant design

of a bottle of Chanel N°5. Both objects made a vivid impression on Yeoh and in her eyes, they are irresistible to draw.

Yeoh's interpretations of iconic Chanel designs reflect the spark of joy she feels – and undoubtedly many women feel too – when they see the beauty, elegance and imagination of a Chanel creation, whether in ready-to-wear, couture, watches, jewellery or fragrance.

With soft pencil touches and by making expressive use of blank space and fine lines, Yeoh brings an effortless feel to her virtuoso, swift live drawing and sketches. Her work is easily legible yet always has a unique creative twist: a knowing smile, a leg crossed just-so, a witty use of lettering. Yeoh also loves to bring Miss Mimi to life – a story character and constant companion who radiates personality, combining a classic elegance with playful charm. A joy to behold, Miss Mimi embodies the freedom-loving, independent spirit associated with Gabrielle Chanel, connecting the dots in Yeoh's creative world.

THE HOUSE OF CHANEL FOUND ITS WAY ONTO YEOH'S RADAR WHEN SHE WAS 15 YEARS OLD

The illustrator loves to bring Miss Mimi to life, a story character and constant companion who radiates personality

THE CHANEL
25 HANDBAG

*Yeoh likes to incorporate elements like textures, colours
and even swatches from make-up into an illustration*

JENNY CHUI

CHANEL

ILLUSTRATED

Jerry chui
the profile

Event and fashion styling, digital visual creation and more – Jenny Chui is a multifaceted creative for whom fashion illustration is both the foundation of her talent and the wellspring of her artistic output. The seeds of those interests were planted early on, as she already loved drawing from the age of four. As a child, she often spent time at her grandmother's, where there weren't many toys – so, she entertained herself with pencils and markers. Later, Japanese anime caught her attention, especially the characters in *Sailor Moon*, who always wore beautiful outfits. In high school, fashion made its entrance. Inspired by the models in magazine clippings, she started drawing girls in fashionable outfits.

Chui pursued a bachelor's degree in fashion design and later completed a PhD in fashion and technology from Hong Kong Polytechnic University. She created countless sketches there with the goal of developing fashion collections. But despite her first-class honours, the experience made her see her true passion more clearly. Chui enjoyed the process of drawing, sketching and illustrating much more than draping fabric or sewing garments. Meanwhile, a former classmate who'd become a fashion reporter enlisted her for a live drawing event at a time when that wasn't a very common thing to do. More commissions followed. The notion solidified in Chui's mind that a career as a fashion designer wasn't the way forward. She set up a small studio as a fashion illustrator to keep up with demand and branched out from drawing fashion portraits in real time to creating visuals for magazines, hotels and other clients.

Chanel Beauty was one of them, paving the way for Chanel Watches and Chanel Fine Jewellery. Chui feels much affinity with Chanel's house codes. Black plays a crucial role in her bold and striking illustrations, which use a limited amount of colour to express silhouettes. Instead, she favours clean lines and negative space, allowing the imagination to run free. Black, in the same vein as Gabrielle Chanel used it, also symbolises

a classic and powerful elegance to Chui. Each time she integrates the house's iconic symbols in her work – N°5, the comet, the lion – the illustrator recognises that working with Chanel, and meeting the brand's high standards, is no small feat.

That's why Chui revels the most in the process. She approaches her illustration like Chanel approaches the craftsmanship of its products: with emotion and passion that turns the result into something truly luxurious. Chanel's clients, she notices, often commit to a total fashion statement. They wear the prêt-à-porter or couture outfits head-to-toe; they apply the fragrance and use the make-up. The total look radiates elegance, deepening her attraction to drawing women in the brand's silhouettes. Once, Chui single-handedly started a personal challenge, titling it 'Ten Days of Drawing Chanel'. It wasn't hard to find material to work with at all, affirming Chui's belief that you can never run out of inspiration when it comes to illustrating Chanel.

BLACK, IN THE SAME VEIN AS GABRIELLE CHANEL USED IT, SYMBOLISES A CLASSIC AND POWERFUL ELEGANCE TO CHUI

Jerrychui
the profile

CHANEL

CHANEL

CHANEL

CHANEL

*The artist approaches her illustration like Chanel
approaches the craftsmanship of its products*

Jerry chui
the profile

Inspired by the models in magazine clippings, the illustrator started drawing girls in fashionable outfits

JOANNA LAYLA

CHANEL

ILLUSTRATED

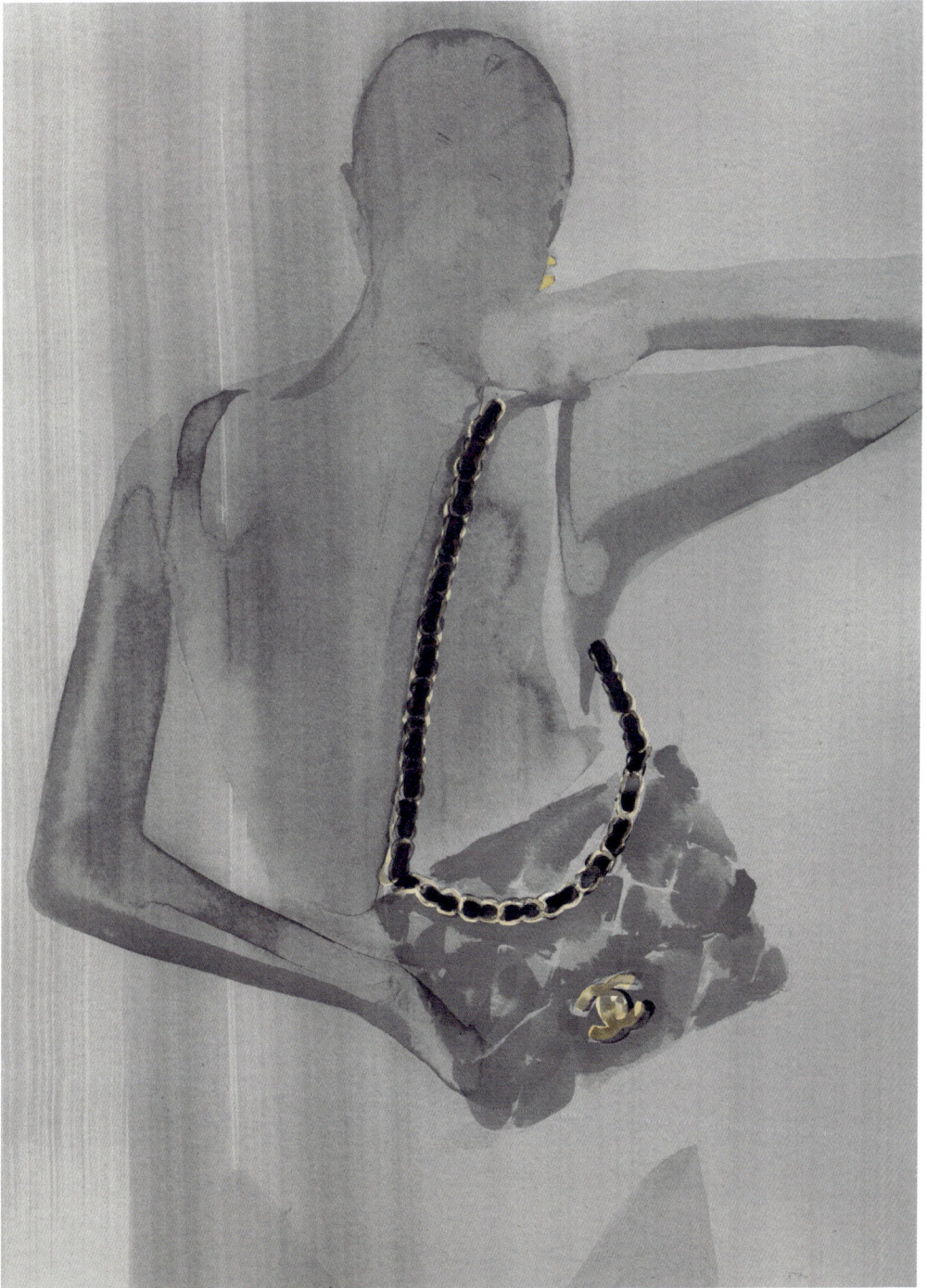

Drawing has always been something of an instinct for Joanna Layla. The London-based illustrator recalls immersing herself in the activity – it's one of her earliest memories.

Both surprisingly and tellingly, Layla went on to study literature at university. But not just any literature – illuminated manuscripts were her specialisation, uncannily anticipating her future career as a visual storyteller. You could say that, in an illuminated manuscript from the Middle Ages or Renaissance, the words are dancing on the page, accompanied as they are by intricate embellishments – not to mention illustrations – that add visual richness to the text. When she showed a tutor from Central Saint Martins her drawings, he gave her eye-opening feedback. He saw that she was an illustrator at heart. Those words changed something within her.

But even though Layla always had her own signature line and style, she mainly continued to draw for herself, developing her craft on her own. When she became a mother, in the act of creating a life, her creative artist's instinct, too, gained strength. She credits that time – in which she became fearless and excited to create again – with allowing her work to come into its own. When Layla leaned into what she loved, everything fell into place. Clients in the fashion, beauty and lifestyle realms quickly followed.

Fashion, in particular, resonates with Layla. She's fascinated with how people choose to express themselves through clothes and how fashion functions as a visual expression of identity. She feels most creative and inspired in that environment: working with designers, stylists and fashion editors. The designers that have influenced Layla the most are those who created a unique visual language with their designs, such as Gabrielle Chanel, Phoebe Philo, Yves Saint Laurent and Dries Van Noten. She looks up to fashion image makers like Viviane Sassen, Alexandra Carl and Inez & Vinoodh, and artists like Louise Bourgeois, Cecily Brown, Marlene Dumas and Katinka Lampe.

In Layla's body of work, those influences are plentiful in incredibly subtle ways. The dark ink figures that loom large in her aesthetic are reminiscent of Sassen's use of shadows. The influence of motherhood is very Bourgeois. And the simplicity and elegance of her monochrome illustrations read both very Philo and very Gabrielle Chanel. One of Chanel's personal mottos – 'Always to take off, never to add' – is a common thread in Layla's work, whose images explore the power of simplifying things in order to articulate an idea all the more powerfully.

Gabrielle Chanel didn't sketch her designs on paper, but she designed her silhouettes by draping and cutting fabrics directly onto models. This leaves a perfect space for artists and illustrators to capture and interpret the vision of Chanel, Layla has always found. Whether she's drawing from Chanel's 'Les Métiers d'Art' collections every fashion week, or working on 'Drawing Chanel' for the Victoria and Albert Museum, pulling from Chanel's archives, Layla portrays that legendary vision in her own way, over and over again.

ONE OF CHANEL'S PERSONAL MOTTOS – 'ALWAYS TO TAKE OFF, NEVER TO ADD' – IS A COMMON THREAD IN LAYLA'S WORK

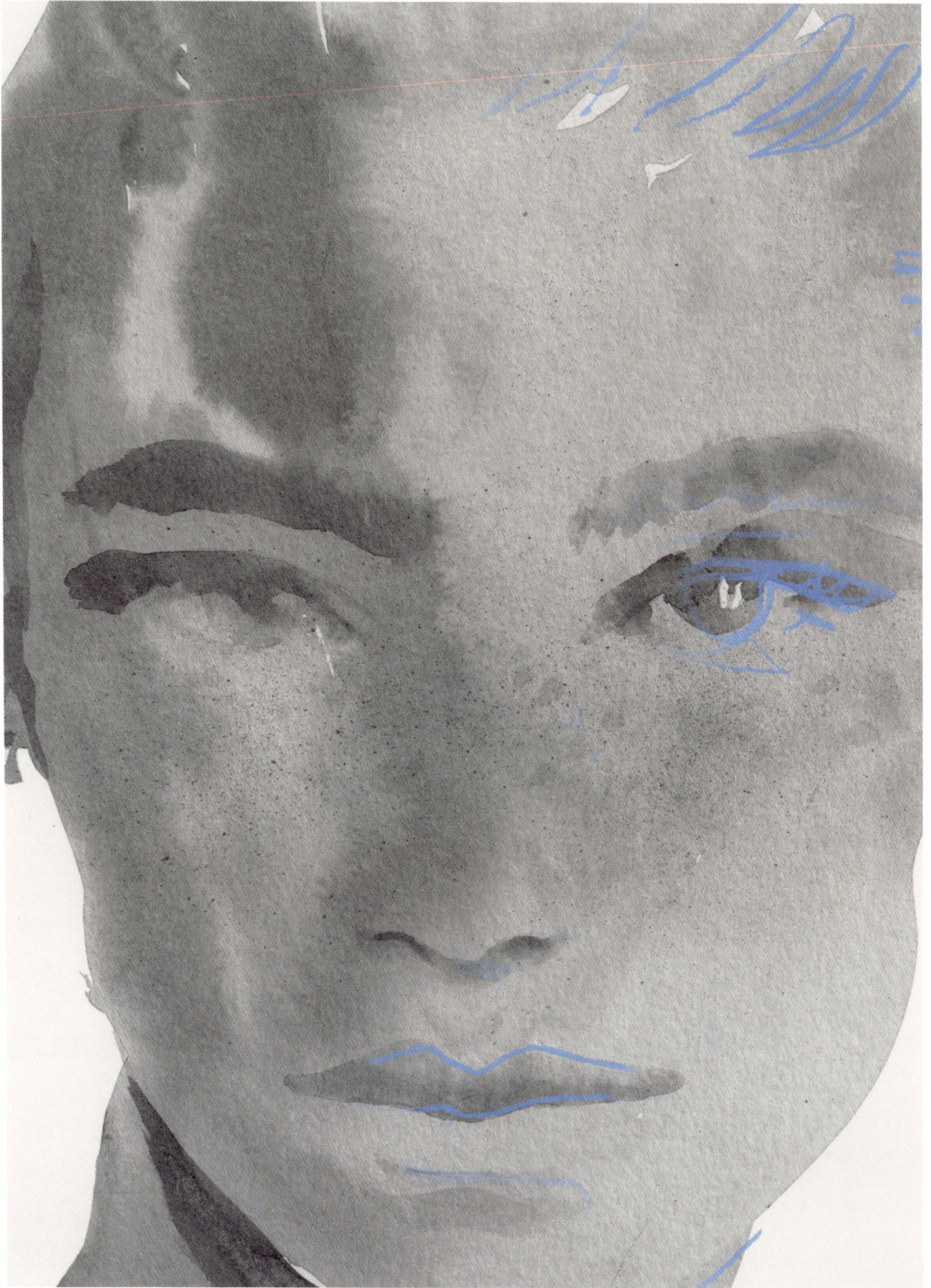

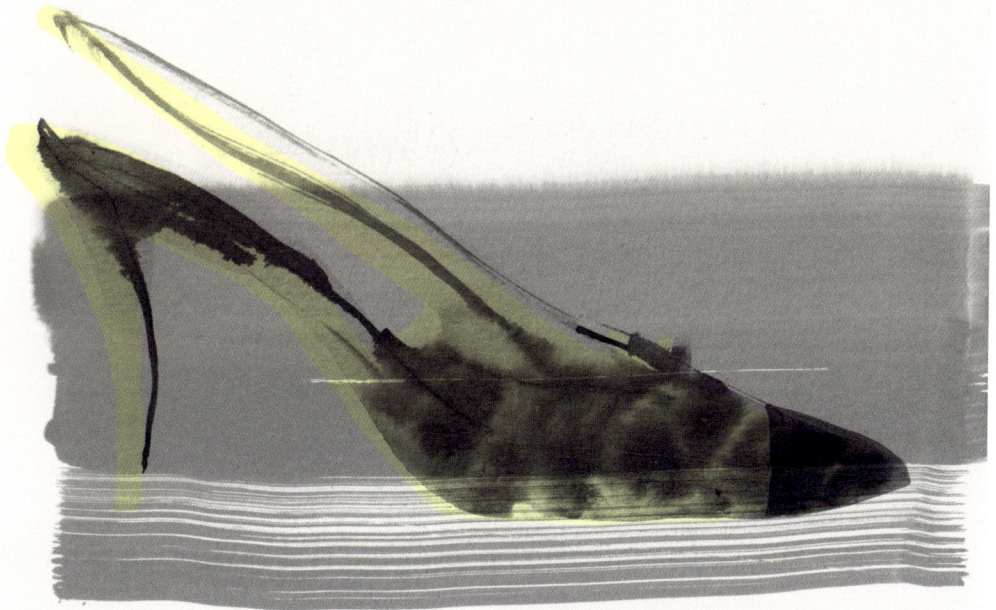

*Layla's images explore the power of simplifying things in
order to articulate an idea all the more powerfully*

The artist is fascinated with how people choose to express themselves through clothes and how fashion functions as a visual expression of identity

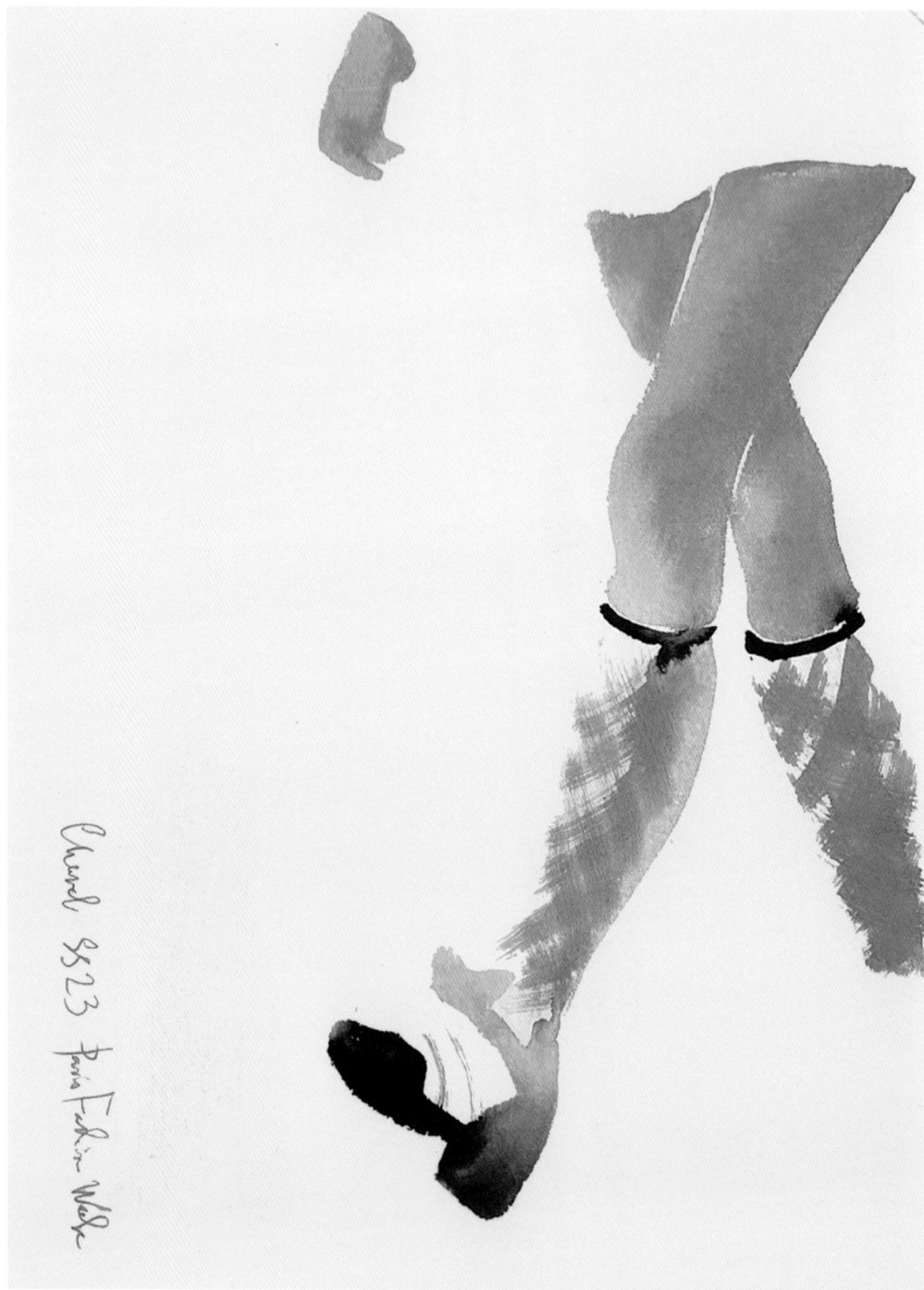

Chanel 8523 Paris Fashion Week

Chanel 8523 Paris Fashion Week

KAROLINA PAWELCZYK

CHANEL

ILLUSTRATED

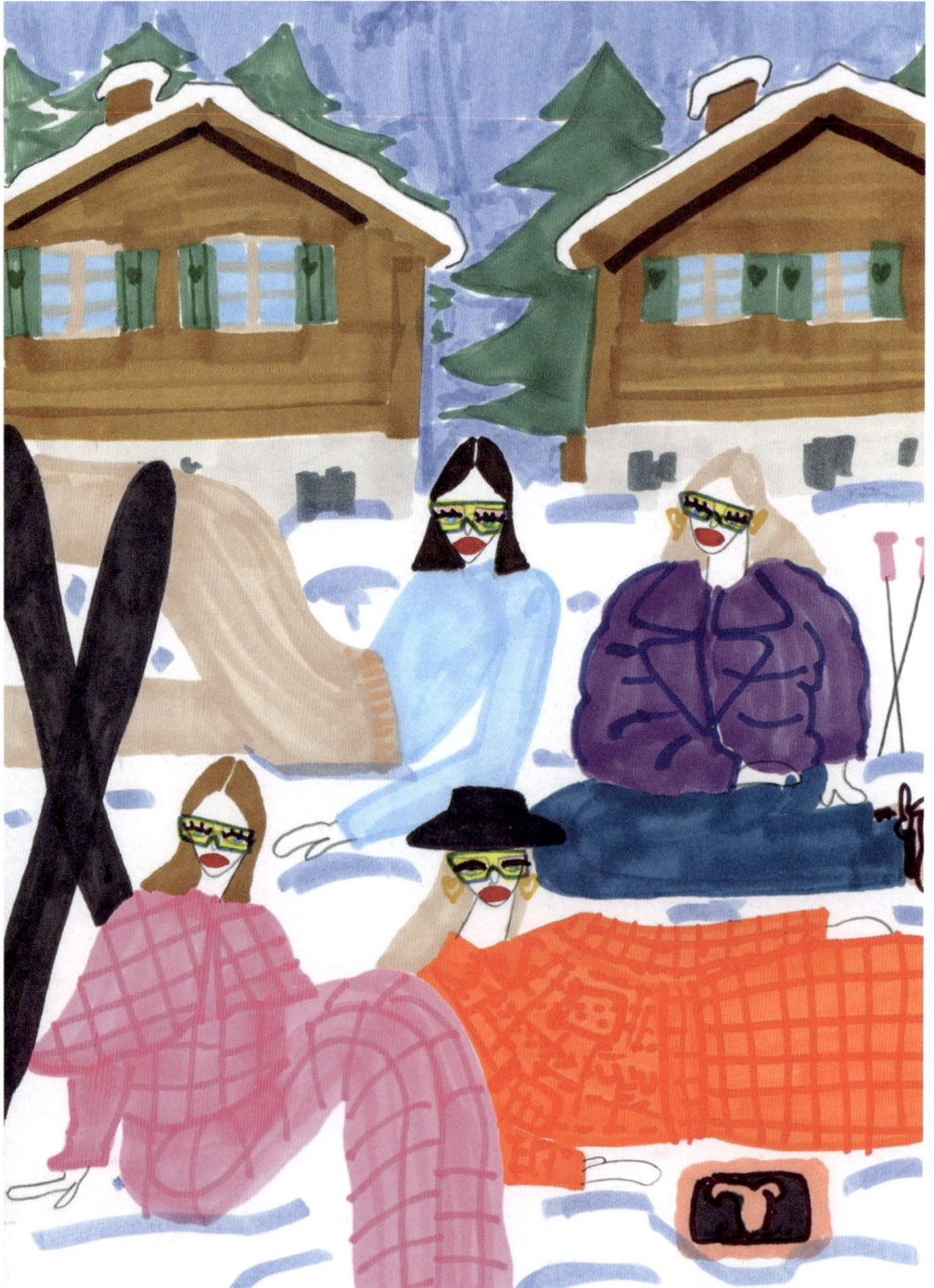

Karolina Pawelczyk loves to learn about what drives luminaries in different fields – from artists to athletes. By reading their biographies, the Polish illustrator discovers different angles to their work, which encourages her to develop an idiosyncratic way of thinking when creating her own art.

Pawelczyk's creative life started as a child, when she and her twin sister would come up with imaginative games. They enthusiastically set up photo shoots for their dachshund Saba and the duo would stage plays that their whole family just *had* to attend – they even made posters for their productions. Pawelczyk's eye for graphics and drawing continued to evolve from this fertile ground.

In her primary school art classes, she simply enjoyed all they had to offer, from putting together exhibitions, to going on painting excursions. It all felt like a natural fit. Later, Pawelczyk initially enrolled in law school in Poland. Yet, at the same time, her love of drawing kept growing. She almost couldn't help herself from continuing to look for ways to develop her skills further. London was calling – more specifically, a fashion illustration course at Central Saint Martins.

For Pawelczyk, living and studying in the British capital opened new creative horizons and encouraged her to have fun with her drawings. That sense of playfulness and levity remains a vibrant presence in the illustrator's work today. Like the expressive colours that Pawelczyk finds so captivating in the work of other artists – from Picasso's sketches to André Butzer's offbeat characters – so too does the Polish illustrator's own artwork exude a high-frequency energy driven by colour and a childlike simplicity of form.

Pawelczyk's use of coloured pencils and vivid markers on white backgrounds as a canvas reinforces this sense of play. Her figures jump off the page or screen, with her frequent use of an-imation fittingly enhancing that dynamism. She has created elaborate illustrations for boutique windows that enliven shopping street façades with her girly dreamworlds, and conjured city scenes populated with her joyful characters on to-go coffee cups. Whatever the brand collaboration calls for, Pawelczyk's work is guaranteed to add a vibrant charm and funky personality.

Pawelczyk's fantasy world has parallels with the Chanel Spring-Summer 1995 Ready-to-Wear collection by Karl Lagerfeld, which is unsurprisingly her absolute favourite to draw. The Barbie pinks (and fuchsias, oranges and reds!), the dollhouse vibe of the catwalk scenography and the confident smiles inspire her endlessly. Chanel perfume bottles, bags and shoes, too, in their simplicity and beauty, often figure in her sketches. For Pawelczyk, it's about that entire Chanel universe: the bright red lip that's both classic and daring, the bubblegum pink tweed suit made to move around and have fun in, a relaxed but stylish way of being, just as Gabrielle Chanel envisioned it when she liberated women from the restrictive corset. Pawelczyk's women – stylised, long limbed and slightly disproportionate – live in a universe of lightness and brightness. The world is their playground, too, and they live in it with heaps of attitude.

PAWELCZYK'S FANTASY WORLD HAS PARALLELS WITH KARL LAGERFELD'S SPRING-SUMMER 1995 READY-TO-WEAR COLLECTION

The Polish illustrator's artwork exudes a high-frequency
energy driven by colour and a childlike simplicity of form

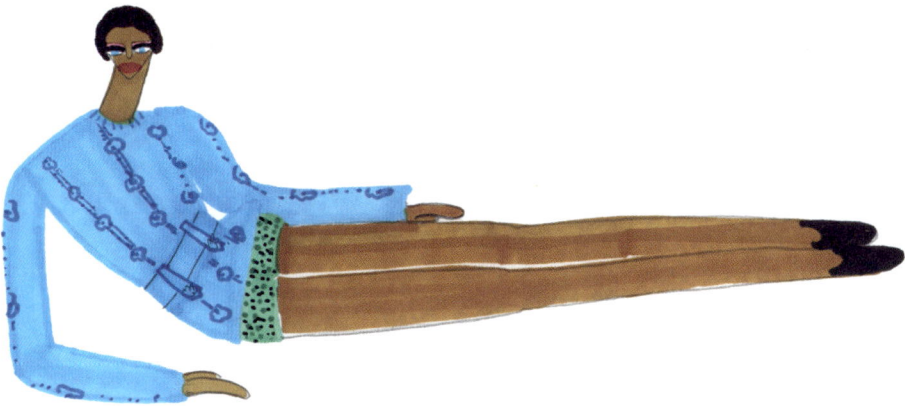

*Pawelczyk's women – stylised, long limbed and slightly
disproportionate – live in a universe of lightness and brightness*

KELLY SMITH

CHANEL

ILLUSTRATED

While a student of photography and graphic design at the School of Creative Arts and Media at the University of Tasmania, Kelly Smith discovered that it was possible to make her favourite pastime into a successful career. Though she originally intended to find work in publishing as an editorial designer or photographer, she became fascinated with the more commercial side of illustration.

The Australian illustrator tapped into her talent for drawing and fantasy early on. As a child, she had a vivid imagination and felt the magnetism of the world of make-believe. Drawing allowed her to create entire worlds on paper. When she encountered the elaborate fashion show productions of Chanel, she was amazed. The French maison's Spring-Summer 2009 Haute Couture show especially – set in an all-white room decorated with giant paper flowers like camellias and roses in which models came down the runway in squared-off silhouettes complete with precision-cut paper headdresses in floral designs by the Japanese milliner, hairstylist and artist Katsuya Kamo – gave her the itch to begin sketching right away.

A fashion editorial by Hamish Bowles Smith had seen a few years before, in the December 2003 issue of American *Vogue*, had a similar effect. Photographed by Annie Leibovitz and styled by Grace Coddington, it staged a particularly fashion-forward interpretation of the wondrous world of the 1865 children's novel *Alice's Adventures in Wonderland* by Lewis Carroll. Especially the image featuring Karl Lagerfeld in his iconic black and white suit, standing in a field beside Natalia Vodianova as Alice, stuck with her. For Smith, few moments are more potent than when fashion and art collide.

The influence of fairy tales, fashion and dreamlike worlds is palpable in Smith's aesthetic. Her style of illustrating is feminine and delicate, with a touch of playfulness that finds parallels with the whimsy she found so inspiring in her encounters with Chanel's catwalk productions under the creative direction of Karl Lagerfeld. When illustrating Chanel, Smith makes use of an elevated simplicity. She favours a monochrome palette, sometimes inflected with pops of colour, but mostly making use of soft shading and fluid lines that reveal the talent of an illustrator most at home with a pencil in her hand. This includes an Apple Pencil. When Smith makes use of digital tools, she enjoys being able to work directly in colour without compromising the process.

Smith feels a kinship with Lagerfeld, who could be considered an illustrator at heart. The German fashion designer, who was appointed creative director at Chanel in 1983 and remained there until his death in 2019, had an extraordinary ability to sketch off the cuff. He left behind hundreds of drawings – concepts brought to life by the talented artisans at Chanel's ateliers, as well as improvised designs or likenesses of the personalities surrounding him. In Smith's view, her own practice – rooted in the creative force that is fashion – owes much to that approach: like art imitating art imitating life.

WHEN ILLUSTRATING CHANEL, SMITH MAKES USE OF AN ELEVATED SIMPLICITY

Smith feels a kinship with Lagerfeld, who could be considered an illustrator at heart

The influence of fairy tales, fashion and dream-like worlds is palpable in Smith's aesthetic

LENA
KER

CHANEL
ILLUSTRATED

For Lena Ker, drawing is about continuous learning, experimenting, and finding her own voice through practice. The self-taught illustrator remembers how her love for drawing started as a child, and was encouraged when even at that tender age she received praise.

At the time, she dreamt of becoming a famous fashion designer. But she quickly realised that it wasn't the core skills of a designer, like sewing or pattern-making, that attracted her to that profession – it was the imaginative sketching that captivated her. Once she realised the magnitude of the field of illustration, her mind was made up. Ker started a blog on Blogspot that launched her in an organic way, and she steadily began gaining clients.

Today, when she collaborates with fashion brands, what Ker loves the most is the sense of being a part of something bigger and creating a shared vision of creativity and style. Seeing her work enhance a brand's message and helping bring ideas to life through a shared creative process is both rewarding and inspiring to the Russian illustrator.

When she started out, Ker was deeply inspired by well-known names like David Downton. Then, she became more focused on developing her own unique style. In her work, which ranges from illustration to animation and watercolour, Ker strives to capture realism and beauty. Her style focuses on classical anatomical traditions and bold colours, and reflects her admiration for timeless elegance, grace and femininity.

The Chanel looks that attract Ker time and time again are those from the 1990s, a time of supermodels, glamour, bold fashions and attitude. Her illustrations that are inspired by this era convey a sense of rhythm, of dynamism: of women who enjoy a life well lived and simply happen to be wearing fabulous clothes. Two of her absolute favourite shows are the Chanel Spring-Summer 1992 Ready-to-Wear Collection, a pop-culture

classic with brightly coloured tweed skirt suits and oversized chains, and the Spring-Summer 1997 Haute Couture show, a more demure black and white collection featuring veiled wide-brim hats and gloves. Both references demonstrate the irresistible attraction of Chanel. The French house embodies a perfect juxtaposition between femininity's polar opposites – energetic playfulness and towering strength.

Ker's watercolours, included in this book, are slightly softer versions of her signature aesthetic, more tentative and sketched, with looser lines and dreamier colours. The choice for the medium was driven by the light and fluid brush strokes, which the illustrator feels work beautifully to capture the elegance of the French house. Ker wanted the illustrations to feel soft yet precise, evoking a sense of classic luxury that resonates with Chanel's identity.

More than that, Ker feels a strong connection with Chanel founder and namesake Gabrielle 'Coco' Chanel, a fiercely independent designer. She's deeply impressed by both Gabrielle Chanel's personal journey and the revolution the trailblazing legend brought to the world of fashion. It's only fitting for an illustrator whose passion for drawing has enabled her to carve out a creative space for herself, too.

KER FEELS A STRONG CONNECTION WITH CHANEL FOUNDER GABRIELLE CHANEL, A FIERCELY INDEPENDENT DESIGNER

The choice for watercolours was driven by the light and fluid brush strokes, which the illustrator feels work beautifully to capture the elegance of the French house

LYDIA
BOURHILL

CHANEL

ILLUSTRATED

Chanel

Time and travel. These two elements have propelled Lydia Bourhill's practice as an illustrator over the years. The Scottish artist's penchant for drawing grew in proportion to the experiences and journeys she collected as student and teenager. Deeply interested in languages, music and the arts, Bourhill pursued musical training and European adventures – even living in Spain for a time – all the while capturing moments on paper in a spontaneous way. Over the years, her talent blossomed.

Bourhill recalls a breakthrough moment one evening when she stayed late at university in Edinburgh, where she was studying illustration and visual communication. She had the department to herself and began experimenting freely with inks, textiles and water-based media. That night, through an introspective creative process of trial and error, Bourhill discovered her signature style – elegant, loose and layered, with a vintage feel.

In Bourhill's illustrations, you can sense the influence of the animated storytelling capacities of Quentin Blake and Ludwig Bemelmans, whose styles she finds inspiring. But there are also discernible traces of the restrained yet feminine aesthetic of some of fashion's greats, like Cecil Beaton, Christian Dior and Gabrielle Chanel. Ever a reference, Bourhill often looks to Chanel's seminal 1959 haute couture show for its exemplary modern elegance. In the fifties, Chanel launched the iconic 2.55 handbag, perfected the timeless tweed skirt suit with black ribbon trim, and focused on streamlined silhouettes with a minimum of embellishment – except for the brand's trademark abundantly layered faux pearl necklaces.

'It was my good fortune to realise early that simplicity is elegance.' This quote by Gabrielle Chanel encapsulates the illustrator's approach perfectly. Like Chanel, Bourhill likes to keep things classic. Using black chalk, watercolour and ink for the artwork featured in this book, she makes use of limited, purposeful strokes to create simple yet refined renderings of iconic Chanel accessories and silhouettes.

In 2024, Bourhill was commissioned to create illustrations for The Kensington Hotel's 'High Fashion High Tea', a special afternoon tea in honour of the *Gabrielle Chanel. Fashion Manifesto* exhibition at the Victoria and Albert Museum in London. It was a whimsical way to capture the essence of Chanel – the woman as well as the brand – and take part in a larger creative conversation about the legendary fashion house and its founder.

For Bourhill, who first heard the term 'little black dress' while playing dress-up in her mother's evening clothes as a young girl, collaborating with luxury brands in fashion, jewellery, hospitality and travel ties together all of her passions. Today, as a successful creative visualiser, Bourhill loves using her talents in the field of luxury. Whether observing an Italian cobblestone street, an atmospheric bar in Mayfair, the crisp skyline of Chicago or the accoutrements of a French Riviera holiday, the process of capturing the world around her takes Bourhill back to that earlier process of committing to paper travel and life experiences while immersed in creative solitude.

'IT WAS MY GOOD FORTUNE TO REALISE EARLY THAT SIMPLICITY IS ELEGANCE.' LIKE CHANEL, BOURHILL LIKES TO KEEP THINGS CLASSIC

The artist makes use of limited, purposeful strokes to create simple yet refined renderings of iconic Chanel accessories and silhouettes

MILA
GISLON

CHANEL
ILLUSTRATED

The extroverted street style of the Milanese is a unique amalgamation of art and fashion. It caught the youthful eye of Mila Gislon, who grew up in Milan absorbing the fashion capital's rich visual culture. She loved spending her free time drawing, and always knew that the intersection of fashion and art was exactly where she wanted to direct her own artistic focus.

Gislon applied herself to painting realistic portraiture and practising anatomy drawing, a combination that mimicked classical training and that she credits with shaping her work to this day. Then, using that foundation, she followed in the footsteps of artists who subverted that training to find their own voice. Experimenting her way to honing her own point of view, Gislon was poised to make a splash. When she was in high school, the digital drawing app Procreate featured her work on its social media channels. The incredible public response she received helped Gislon take her passion more seriously.

The Italian fashion illustrator's work is bold and almost abstracted – making use of strong planes of saturated colour, blown-up florals and fine-line detailing to trace models' silhouettes and foreground textile patterns. The romanticism that she adores in Paolo Roversi's work finds its way into her drawings via dark moody figures and blooms that blend into the surroundings, while the free and playful forms of Hilma af Klint find their parallel in Gislon's use of a vibrant spectrum of red, purples and pinks.

Closer to home, she credits her grandmother Jeanette, a woman with an amazing eye and sense of style, for always giving her a fresh perspective on her art. It was Jeanette who commented on a knitted jacket – with black lace and pearls – Gislon bought as a young girl, referring to it as her 'Chanel jacket'. Gislon recalls being instantly attracted to a Karl Lagerfeld illustration of Gabrielle Chanel in a book, sensing an instant connection to the strong, sharp-looking, elegant woman depicted and wanting to find

out more about who she was and how she lived her life. The illustrator continues to find inspiration in the sense of freedom and emancipated, fearless femininity that Chanel has stood for since the house's founding in 1910. That timeless quality leads Gislon to draw Chanel pieces – again and again.

The symbolism of visual storytelling through illustration weaves its way through Gislon's love for fashion illustration and fashion photography as she encountered it in the work of George Barbier, Guy Bourdin and Mats Gustafson. And when a fashion story is set in a fanciful context, like a catwalk show's scenography or a fashion editorial, it activates Gislon's radar for story-driven imagery.

Take the Chanel Cruise 2012/13 collection, for example, which took place in Versailles. With its flirty, frivolous pastel A-line skirts in both long and micro versions, layered ruffles, gorgeous jewels and satin ribbons in models' hair reminiscent of Rococo paintings by Fragonard, it remains one of Gislon's favourites.

GISLON CONTINUES TO FIND INSPIRATION IN THE SENSE OF FREEDOM AND EMANCIPATED, FEARLESS FEMININITY THAT CHANEL HAS STOOD FOR SINCE THE HOUSE'S FOUNDING

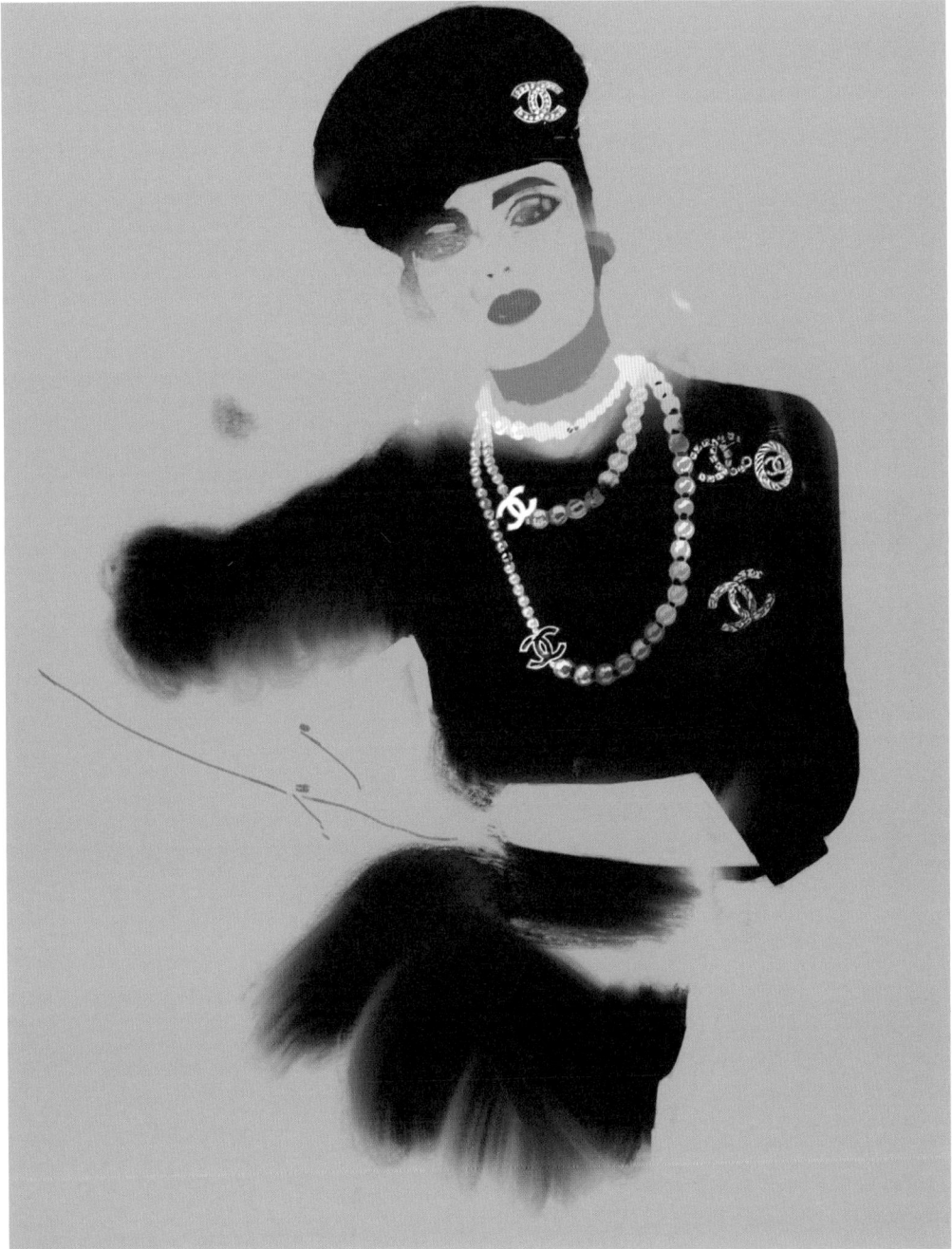

*Mila Gislon grew up in Milan absorbing the
fashion capital's rich visual culture*

The free and playful forms of Hilma af Klint find their parallel in Gislon's use of a vibrant spectrum of red, purples and pinks

The Italian fashion illustrator's work is bold and almost abstracted – making use of strong planes of saturated colour, blown-up florals and fine-line detailing

*The symbolism of visual storytelling through illustration weaves
its way through Gislon's love for fashion illustration*

MIYUKI
OHASHI

CHANEL
ILLUSTRATED

MIYUKI OHASHI
Croquis №

CHANEL

MÉTIERS
D'ART
PARIS-
SALZBURG

In Miyuki Ohashi's illustrations, meaning and movement are created by what she has chosen to leave out, just as much as by what she has deftly put in. A coloured marker in a single zigzag line denotes a model's vivacious strut; a line break disrupts the symmetry of a face, leaving the viewer to fill in arresting features. There's a simplicity that belies the mastery – and the practice it takes to perfect what looks like a rapid-fire sketch.

In fact, the Japanese illustrator has been drawing for as long as she can remember. Before she even discovered fashion illustration, she was naturally drawn to it, sketching girls dressed in stylish outfits. But she also pursued other activities, such as sports and music. When the time came to attend university, Ohashi chose to study French, further developing her well-rounded set of interests. That formative feeling of simply loving to sketch, however, never left her. So, Ohashi decided to pursue her passion. She enrolled in Setsu Mode Seminar, an avant-garde art and fashion school in Tokyo, founded by Setsu Nagasawa, a pioneering Japanese fashion illustrator.

An influential figure in Japanese visual culture, Nagasawa was renowned for his expressive, fluid line work and minimalist watercolour technique. His school, which closed in 2017, nurtured generations of manga artists, fashion designers and illustrators – including Ohashi, who counts Nagasawa and her other teachers there among her greatest mentors and inspirations. The experience gave her both the confidence and the foundational training to consider illustration as a serious career path.

Ohashi recalls regularly illustrating catwalk looks during her classes at Setsu Mode Seminar. In those moments, she often looked to Chanel almost instinctively. She finds that the brand's iconic presence feels almost eternal, as if it has always existed at the heart of the fashion world. Ohashi admires the French

house's signature blend of timeless elegance and ever-evolving freshness, as witnessed in the brand's long-time creative director Karl Lagerfeld's decades of inventive seasonal renewal. Ohashi aims to radiate that dynamism through her own visual language as well – and she does so with brio.

Like Nagasawa, Ohashi's hand-drawn lines create simplified forms whose fluidity evokes a sense of bold creative freedom. Stylised and loosely composed, the silhouettes she draws are buzzing with energy and motion. Rendered in her favourite media – pencil, marker and acrylic paint – Ohashi chooses certain materials for their varying textures and capacity to express different qualities in different settings. A printed booklet that accompanied her 2021 solo exhibition 'Mood', for example, invited viewers to experience her drawings' original textures through stencil printing. And within the realm of fashion brands, among other projects, Ohashi has created illustrations for window displays, in-store displays and events.

In essence, illustrating fashion means more than just celebrating clothes in themselves to Ohashi. The art form allows her to pay homage to the elegance, strength and subtle beauty that she recognises in people – all by harnessing the power of line and colour.

OHASHI FINDS THAT CHANEL'S ICONIC PRESENCE FEELS ALMOST ETERNAL, AS IF IT HAS ALWAYS EXISTED AT THE HEART OF THE FASHION WORLD

CHANEL

MIYUKI OHASHI
Croquis No

MIYUKI OHASHI
Croquis N⁰_____

Before she even discovered fashion illustration, Ohashi was naturally drawn to it, sketching girls dressed in stylish outfits

CHANEL, PARIS IN ROME 2015/16
MÉTIERS D'ART

MIYUKI OHASHI
Croquis No

Stylised and loosely composed, the silhouettes Ohashi
draws are buzzing with energy and motion

Karl
Lagerfeld

CHANEL
2023/24
MÉTIERS
D'ART
SHOW
MANCHESTER
MCR

*Ohashi enrolled in an avant-garde art and fashion school in Tokyo
founded by Setsu Nagasawa, a pioneering Japanese fashion illustrator*

NICOLE JARECZ

CHANEL

ILLUSTRATED

It takes innate talent and intentional, continuous exploration of your craft to master the kind of style Nicole Jarecz' drawing practice has evolved into over the last 15 years.

The Michigander remembers filling sketchbooks as a child and loving the challenge of having sketch competitions with friends and family members. When her father took her on weekly visits to a local bookstore as a teenager, she discovered fashion books and *Vogue* magazine. She studied both endlessly.

But it didn't cross Jarecz' mind that her favourite pastime could become a career until her high school art teacher suggested she consider going to art college. Motivated, she prepared a portfolio during her final year and was accepted on a scholarship to attend Detroit's top-ranked College for Creative Studies, or CCS.

Though Jarecz' interest in illustration undoubtedly grew while she studied at CCS, she feels strongly that other formative life experiences have made her into the illustrator she is today. One of those major moments includes moving to Paris in her early twenties. At that point Jarecz had already encountered the Chanel brand. Yet, living in the City of Lights suddenly made the allure of the legendary effortlessly chic Parisian woman, which the French maison is closely entwined with, much more tangible. The elegant silhouettes she had admired in those fashion magazines had once felt like a different world – but now she was immersed in that world, and it left an indelible impression on her as an artist.

Over time, Jarecz' work has struck a balance between the more polished style of drawing with much attention to detail and precise lines that she looked up to in René Gruau's work and the gestural, energetic style she admires in Kenneth Paul Block's drawings for *Women's Wear Daily*. Like Block, who used to sketch society ladies in their finest clothes as well as catwalk shows,

Jarecz enjoys the directness of live sketching events, capturing movement and energy in a way that's challenging to accomplish.

Karl Lagerfeld's time at Chanel is especially inspiring to the American illustrator. Lagerfeld infused Chanel with a theatricality that made infinite reinvention possible through his love of youthfulness and humour, while retaining the brand's strong, iconic identity. The sets Lagerfeld would create for the Chanel catwalk shows are testament to that vision: from the Arctic environment he created, complete with a monumental iceberg towering over the audience in 2009 for the Fall-Winter 2009/10 Ready-to-Wear collection, to the seaside escape that brought a real sandy beach to the historic Grand Palais in Paris in 2018 for the Spring-Summer 2019 Ready-to-Wear collection. The feeling, the fantasy – that was the point.

When Jarecz illustrates Chanel, she strives to capture something more than fashion, too. Her effortless lines, the dreamy gaze of her figures, the contrasting backgrounds and impactful use of negative space convey an idea beyond clothes – they suggest a mood, a dream, the essence of the brand. They encapsulate the elegance of true style that Jarecz once observed in Paris, shaped by Chanel and brought to life through her art.

LIVING IN PARIS MADE THE ALLURE OF THE EFFORTLESSLY CHIC PARISIAN WOMAN, WHICH CHANEL IS CLOSELY ENTWINED WITH, MORE TANGIBLE

Jarecz enjoys the directness of live sketching events, capturing movement and energy in a way that's challenging to accomplish

*When Jarecz illustrates Chanel, she strives
to capture something more than fashion*

NINA
COSFORD

CHANEL

ILLUSTRATED

The English Look

CERISE YARN BRAID

CERISE RIBBON

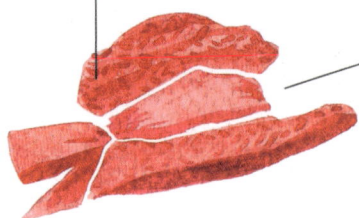

PHEASANT
FEATHERS

STRAW
HAT

DELFT BLUE BEADS

WHITE
GEORGETTE
CRÊPE

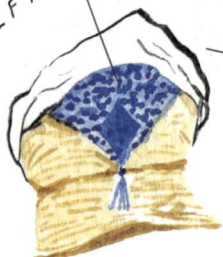

BRAIDED WOOL

BLACK SATIN

MADE OF BLUE AND
BLACK RIBBON

Even though Nina Cosford doesn't remember a life without drawing and always knew she'd go to art school, she was never entirely sure that it could be an actual job, let alone a wildly successful career. When she was younger, she used drawing as a way to escape or pass the time, inventing new worlds as a means of self-expression.

She enrolled in an art foundation course, the United Kingdom's preparation for art school, at the University for the Creative Arts Epsom. That year became one of learning and soul-searching. Cosford went back and forth between believing in herself as a creative – and not. The self-disciplined illustrator, who says her work ethic borders on the obsessive, now realises it was all part and parcel of getting comfortable with the idea that there is, indeed, something she's very good at. Ultimately, Cosford decided to continue to pursue her art education, completing a bachelor's degree in illustration and animation at Kingston University London.

The mental balancing act Cosford became familiar with in school – that fruitful push and pull between self-criticism and self-belief – has become integral to her creative process, propelling her gift forward. The theme is eloquently represented in her work, shining through the personal and societal subjects she likes to broach through her illustration. Cosford's drawings are filled with colourful personalities who relate the imperfections and challenges in the daily life of a girl. The young women possess an honest relatability injected with a serious sense of humour and touching vulnerability. One day Cosford's girl-centric drawings may explore the reasons for being in a bad mood; another day they may evoke the joys of people-watching in Los Angeles, and yet another time her work may wittily comment on the fashion pitfalls of an oversized winter jumper or of owning too many versions of the same thing.

So, it can be said that fashion figures in Cosford's work, but not in the sense of traditional idealised or glamorous fashion illustration. The illustrator's drawings function rather as a cultural perspective on clothes and the way they can make us feel: restricted or free; cheerful or frustrated. It's fitting that Cosford senses a strong connection with an anecdote from Gabrielle Chanel's life. The fashion trailblazer rejected the silliness and impracticality of corsets and long skirts and instead fashioned herself a pair of trousers, so that she could ride a horse astride, rather than side-saddle. Just as Gabrielle Chanel found freedom appealing, Cosford finds the most value and significance in celebrating the more realistic human qualities that connect us to famous people. Often, those aspects make them much more interesting and three-dimensional. That's what Cosford loves about illustrating Chanel's life and work – capturing the visual essence of the designer as a person, not just as an icon or a brand, and getting to the heart of what makes the most classic Chanel items timeless and as relevant as ever.

WHAT COSFORD LOVES ABOUT ILLUSTRATING CHANEL'S LIFE AND WORK IS CAPTURING THE VISUAL ESSENCE OF THE DESIGNER AS A PERSON, NOT JUST AS AN ICON OR A BRAND

earrings

TWO-
TONE
SHOES

WIDE
TROUSERS

2.55 handbag

STRAW

BOATER

pockets! —

pyjama top

costume jewellery

camelia corsage

TWEED JACKET

BRETON TOP

skirt suit

Little Black Dress

pearl necklace

The illustrator's drawings function as a cultural perspective on clothes and the way they can make us feel

camelias

Coco's

a string of pearls

Boy's portrait

shearing scissors

lipstick

perfume

threads

Atelier

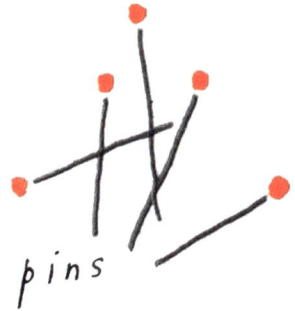

pins

Lion sculpture

bracelets

buttons

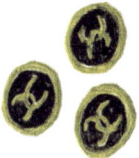

notes

cigarettes

Fashion figures in Cosford's work, but not in the sense of traditional idealised or glamorous fashion illustration

THE "LBD"

'Ecentricity was dying out; I hope,
what's more, that I helped
kill it off' *

*Quote by Gabrielle Chanel

POSUKA
DEMIZU

CHANEL
ILLUSTRATED

A handbag with a shoulder strap, liberating women's movement. A little black dress, the revolutionary new definition of Parisian chic. Two-tone shoes, the finishing touch of a silhouette. For Posuka Demizu, the lauded manga artist and illustrator of *The Promised Neverland* fame, it was a surprise to find out that Gabrielle Chanel was the creator of these designs, which many of us now consider classics. In 2021, Demizu took a deep dive into Chanel history when she was commissioned to create a manga with writer Shirai Kaiu, inspired by the maison's founder Gabrielle Chanel.

Recognised worldwide as a unique form of Japanese culture, manga are comics containing stories presented in episodes, typically printed in black and white. Titled *Miroirs*, the project was accompanied by an exhibition in the Chanel's Ginza, Tokyo tower, which also houses Chanel Nexus Hall, a space for cultural programming in the spirit of Gabrielle Chanel, who was a great supporter of her contemporary creatives in art, music and fashion.

Miroirs, with its subtitle 'Manga meets Chanel', is a story told in three chapters that are reflections of Chanel's pivotal life phases – but set in modern-day Japan and depicted through a protagonist who's not recognisably Gabrielle. (In fact, the third story features a boy who wears red lipstick.) Instead, the evolving main character functions as a hero(ine) representing the multifaceted personality of Chanel, who builds herself up from her disadvantaged schoolgirl days at the convent, where she used her imagination to transport herself to a better future, into an ambitious and visionary woman who loved adventure and chased freedom.

Demizu became enamoured with Chanel's story and spirit through the process of drawing the manga. She sees its storyline as following the arc of many contemporary girls' and women's lives, in which they develop their own style and personality – becoming the heroines of their own stories. And in a post-Chanel world, most women do enjoy certain freedoms that Gabrielle Chanel made possible. Just as Chanel went horse riding in men's garments, the heroine rides a motorcycle. And just like Chanel found love with 'Boy' Capel, who encouraged her talent, the heroine has a love interest, modelled after Tatsuo Kusakabe from *My Neighbor Totoro*.

The heroine metamorphoses throughout the manga's pages – but she's always in a Chanel look surrounded by Chanel elements, for which Demizu let herself be inspired by Chanel's Instagram and her apartment in Paris' 31, Rue Cambon. Demizu admires Chanel's capacity for broadening her horizons. When Chanel was a little girl, isolated and lonely in the convent, she read a lot of novels that fed her imagination. Even as an older lady, Chanel could tap into her mental faculty to travel with the mind through time and space – you might say it was her superpower for survival. This is the crux of the story. By portraying the difficulties we sometimes encounter when diverging from the norm, *Miroirs* is about staying true to oneself – and, like Chanel, possibly ending up changing the world because of it.

DEMIZU BECAME ENAMOURED WITH CHANEL'S STORY AND SPIRIT THROUGH THE PROCESS OF DRAWING THE MANGA *MIROIRS*

*Miroirs is about staying true to oneself – and, like Chanel,
possibly ending up changing the world because of it*

Miroirs, with its subtitle 'Manga meets Chanel', is a story told in three chapters that are reflections of Chanel's pivotal life phases

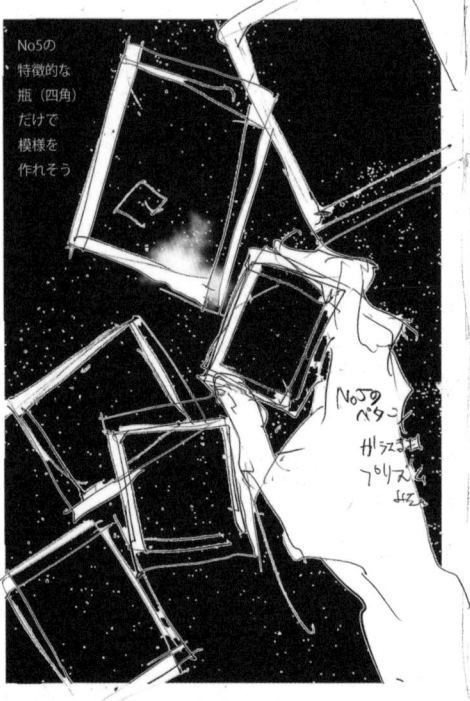

No5の
特徴的な
瓶（四角）
だけで
模様を
作れそう

映画に
出てきた
孤児院の服

上の模様を
配置した
もの

透明感と輝き

考え中

SHAY BEN IZHACK

CHANEL

ILLUSTRATED

COCO
MADEMOISELLE

CHANEL
PARIS

When Shay Ben Izhack was a little girl, she filled the house with her sketches and drawings – often of shoes and purses – and gravitated towards museums and art books. Her mother used to laugh and say that she was born with a paintbrush in her hand. Now, as a mother herself, Ben Izhack's own home is filled with art, too.

She used to dream of becoming a fashion designer, inspired by her aunt who lived in New York City and worked at Ralph Lauren. But as she got older, Ben Izhack realised she was more drawn to illustration and the creative arts than to fashion design itself. She continued making art for herself and her friends, not expecting to find many career opportunities in fashion in Israel. So, Ben Izhack chose a more practical path, studying biology at Tel Aviv University and working as a teacher for some time.

When she was pregnant with her first child, she returned to illustration. By the time she became a mother, she'd made up her mind to set out as an independent artist and fashion illustrator. Of all the international companies she reached out to, Chanel, incredibly to her then, was the first to say yes. The illustration of the Chanel Joaillerie pop-up boutique included in this book was Ben Izhack's very first commission for the French house.

In her art, Ben Izhack often veers from realism towards a more impressionistic style, sometimes with a touch of abstraction. When working with Chanel, she loves blending her signature elements – expressive paint strokes, visible pencil marks, inky blotches and translucent watercolours – with more realistic details. When she sketches catwalk looks, for example, she chooses to reveal the models' faces, a departure from that genre's usual anonymity.

Working with iconic brands like Chanel was beyond anything Ben Izhack imagined as a young girl flipping through the pages of fashion magazines like *Vogue* and *Elle*. Today, as a successful fashion illustrator, she's often given free rein on a variety of creative projects. At live events, she sketches guests and scenes in real time. One of her favourite experiences so far has been illustrating directly onto a product's packaging – transforming each item into a unique, personal, small-scale work of art for guests to take home.

For Ben Izhack, illustration has never felt like work – it's a passion, a dream she feels lucky to have pursued and achieved, even if it meant taking a leap of faith. Leaving behind the stability of teaching wasn't easy, and it required belief not only from herself but also from those closest to her. Looking back, that risk feels entirely worth it. The trust she receives from the brands she collaborates with – and the creative freedom they offer her within their luxurious worlds – is something she never takes for granted. Now, as ever, with that paintbrush in hand, the life she's built allows her to be what she always dreamt of: an artist, fully immersed in the act of creation.

WORKING WITH ICONIC BRANDS LIKE CHANEL WAS BEYOND ANYTHING BEN IZHACK IMAGINED AS A YOUNG GIRL FLIPPING THROUGH FASHION MAGAZINES

Ben Izhack's mother used to laugh and say that
she was born with a paintbrush in her hand

The artist loves blending her signature elements – expressive paint strokes, visible pencil marks, inky blotches and translucent watercolours – with more realistic details

STEVE QUILES

CHANEL

ILLUSTRATED

From an early age, Steve Quiles was attracted to colours, patterns and art. He admired his mother's bottle of Chanel N°5 from afar whenever she was getting ready for a party or special occasion. Attracted by the design's classic squared shape and the perfume's beautiful golden hue, he thought it magical. Quiles' interest in creative, artistic expression was sparked further when he saw Chanel fashions in print for the first time. In a high school fashion illustrator class, one day his art teacher brought in issues of *Women's Wear Daily*. At the time, the fashion industry trade 'bible' was like a colourful folded newspaper, filled with beautiful photographs and fashion illustrations.

With the support of his late mother and art teacher, the born-and-bred New Yorker decided to pursue his passion. He took up painting and started making things out of paper and clay in addition to drawing. After high school, Quiles enrolled in the Fashion Institute of Technology, or FIT, in New York, graduating with two degrees, one in fashion illustration and the other in advertising and design. For the next 24 years, Quiles made a career out of working for major American designer brands as an accessories designer. On the drawing room floor, he always rendered his handbag designs in full detail and loved seeing the pieces come to life, from concept sketch to the leather final product.

The fashion industry was an exciting place to be. But the Covid pandemic, and the time for introspection and creativity it brought, prompted Quiles' illustrator itch to return. Today, he works mainly as a freelance illustrator, creating drawings and art for PR clients and magazines, taking on print and product design commissions, and designing textile prints for brands.

No matter the project, Quiles' illustration style revolves around the mark of the handmade: the brush strokes, watercolours and unique lines of a brush or a pencil. That tactile quality makes the colours and beautiful clothes he interprets in his illustrations stand out and evokes a feeling of beauty in the eye of the beholder.

Given Quiles' penchant for illustrating Chanel, especially the French house's chic brand of classic femininity so glamorously embodied by the supermodels of the 1980s and 90s era, it's no wonder the illustrator first took to drawing Linda Evangelista, Christy Turlington, Gisele Zelauy and Ines de la Fressange walking in the Chanel catwalk shows. In a pre-internet time, he would patiently wait for the magazines to come out. The supermodels' effortless beauty attracted the attention of all; they were women who were aware that all eyes were on them. He was obsessed. It was the fledgling illustrator's first vision of beauty.

Even today, it brings Quiles great pleasure to draw a picture directly onto paper exactly as he sees the image in his mind, and most of all, sharing that idea and feeling of beauty – always with a touch of fantasy – with all of us to admire from up close.

QUILES FIRST TOOK TO DRAWING LINDA EVANGELISTA, CHRISTY TURLINGTON, GISELE ZELAUY AND INES DE LA FRESSANGE WALKING IN THE CHANEL CATWALK SHOWS

The illustrator's style revolves around the mark of the handmade: the
brush strokes, watercolours and unique lines of a brush or a pencil

*Quiles' interest in creative, artistic expression was sparked
when he saw Chanel fashions in print for the first time*

Chanel

Quiles made a career out of working for major American
designer brands as an accessories designer

TANYA CHULKOVA

CHANEL

ILLUSTRATED

When Tanya Chulkova was a little girl at nursery, her parents noticed her knack for drawing. They promptly signed her up for an art club – setting in motion her journey towards becoming a professional fashion illustrator. Glossy magazines became her window into that imaginative and elegant world of fashion, as she spent hours flipping through her mother's collection. She was enchanted and felt as if something that had always been a part of her was ignited.

The Ukrainian illustrator, who now lives in the United Kingdom, went on to study fine art at college. With the rise of social media, Chulkova began sharing her illustrations on Instagram. What started as a spontaneous and unassuming way to share her creative expression led to her work catching the eye of potential clients – among whom, thrillingly, was Chanel.

The French house approached Chulkova with the invitation to illustrate live at a Chanel event during Vogue Fashion's Night Out in Ukraine's capital Kyiv. The event, organised in cities around the world, is a sparkly celebration of style that brings together the leading fashion magazine's editors, models, celebrities and retailers of a city or region. It was Chulkova's very first official commission as a fashion illustrator and the experience was transformative. She decided to take the leap and make a career out of illustration. Since then, the timeless elegance of Chanel has remained a deep source of inspiration in Chulkova's work – with the house's fashion codes a recurring echo of where her personal interest as well as her professional journey began.

Chulkova, who's a virtuoso with Procreate, often starts with a pencil sketch, an initial image where not everything is fully revealed. Then, she may dive further into the details, and use a wide brush to add a softer layer or a blotch of watercolour to create depth. Her lines are always elegant, expressive and feminine. And though rooted in reality, Chulkova's women – impeccably dressed, made up and coiffed – are idealised and reminiscent of the powerful, confident supermodels of the 1980s and 90s. It's a glamorous era that the illustrator often looks to. But Chanel's entire universe, from its couture collections to its costume jewellery, the iconic 11.12 handbag, refined campaign visuals and even the brand's signature make-up powders, fascinate Chulkova with their endless and enduring charms.

And of course, Karl Lagerfeld, the consummate fashion illustration talent who helmed Chanel for over three decades, is a prominent example in Chulkova's drawing practice. His visionary work for Chanel reimagined the spirit of the brand's founder Gabrielle Chanel in every single catwalk show. The way Lagerfeld was able to modernise such a storied brand while remaining reverent to its essence influences Chulkova's approach deeply. Following in the footsteps of the greats she considers the gold standard of fashion illustration, legends like David Downton, Coby Whitmore and Nuno da Costa, Chulkova has forged her own path in the field, finding nuance and refinement with every gesture.

CHANEL'S ENTIRE UNIVERSE, FROM ITS COUTURE COLLECTIONS TO ITS COSTUME JEWELLERY, FASCINATES CHULKOVA WITH ITS ENDLESS AND ENDURING CHARMS

Chulkova's women are idealised and reminiscent of the powerful, confident supermodels of the 1980s and 90s

T.Ch.

*The timeless elegance of Chanel has remained a
deep source of inspiration in Chulkova's work*

VIOLA LI

CHANEL
ILLUSTRATED

Viola Li's love of drawing and her enchantment with illustrating Chanel is inextricably intertwined with memories of her grandmother. She created art, too, and was Li's earliest source of inspiration. As a child, Li's creative gift emerged – drawing, painting and crafting by hand constantly – and was nurtured by her grandmother. It was also through her grandmother's cherished bottle of Chanel N°5 that Li first discovered the iconic French house. The scent of the legendary perfume, at once flowery, powdery and elusive, still has the power to instantly conjure memories of her.

The illustrator, who grew up in Vienna, took art classes as a child and was trained in figurative drawing at the fashion and design high school she attended. That background honed her understanding of visual composition, a solid foundation from which her strong instinct for art and aesthetics could thrive.

In London and Berlin, Li gained valuable experience – in work but also in life, with each city making a profound impression on her and shaping her artistic expression. Upon Li's return to Vienna, she was more than equipped to pursue what she always aspired to: living her life as an artist and attaining a self-determined life as a result of her kaleidoscopic creative journey.

Li's grounding in both Eastern and Western cultures helped crystallise the formative influences that shape her ability to capture subtle emotion, quiet harmony and distinctive beauty – both in her art and in the way she connects with clients.

Today, Li finds inspiration from many different sensory angles: travelling, dancing, music, architecture and interiors, patterns and scents. These interests infuse her illustrations with an elegant dynamism and youthful sophistication. Her line work – minimal yet detailed – reveals the influence of René Gruau, whose boldly elegant images have had a lasting effect on the fashion industry as a whole.

By the same token, the French house of Chanel has played a significant role in Li's choice of subjects and aesthetic evolution. The brand's iconic quilted 2.55 shoulder bag with the interwoven gold chain first sparked the illustrator's desire to translate the Chanel brand's essence onto paper. And Chanel's timeless and elegant silhouettes that exude understated luxury figure in Li's work time and again. Whether capturing a woman walking through a whimsical European city like Vienna or Paris, a pair of models confidently strutting down London's Bond Street in front of Chanel's Christmas windows, or a group of friends donning Halloween costumes amid moody Brooklyn brownstones, the worlds and characters Li brings to life draw the viewer in with their playfulness and energy.

When Li is invited to live-draw guests at brand or private events, she puts that same talent to work to convey her sitter's personality within a distinct atmosphere. With a few confident, fluid pencil strokes and well-chosen colours enhanced with minute details, the illustrator creates an instant rapport – surely, that ability harks back to the deep personal connection she felt with her beloved grandmother.

THE ICONIC QUILTED 2.55 SHOULDER BAG FIRST SPARKED LI'S DESIRE TO TRANSLATE THE CHANEL BRAND'S ESSENCE ONTO PAPER

*Li's line work – minimal yet detailed – reveals
the influence of René Gruau*

*The worlds and characters Li brings to life draw the
viewer in with their playfulness and energy*

*Chanel's timeless and elegant silhouettes that exude
understated luxury figure in Li's work time and again*

pp. 6-17
Anna Blachut
astylishstory.com
@astylishstory

pp. 18-29
Aurore de la Morinerie
auroredelamorinerie.com
@auroredelamorinerie

pp. 30-39
Blair Breitenstein
blairbreitenstein.com
@blairz

pp. 40-49
Cecilia Carlstedt
ceciliacarlstedt.com
@cecilia_carlstedt

pp. 50-59
Chloe Takahashi
chloetakahashi.net
@chloetakahashi_illustrator
pp. 51, 52, 56: © Quarto Publishing /
illustration by Chloe Takahashi

pp. 60-71
Elizabeth Lamb Székely
lizzielambillustration.com
@lizzielambillustration

pp. 72-79
Élodie Clavier Illustration
elodieclavier.com
@elodieclavier_illustrations

pp. 80-91
Gladys Perint Palmer
gladysperintpalmer.com
@gladysperintpalmer

pp. 92-101
Hwi Illust
hwiillust.com
@hwi_illust

pp. 102-109
Jenny Chui
jennytheprofile.com
@jennytheprofile

pp. 110-121
Joanna Layla
joannalayla.com
@joannalayla

pp. 122-131
Karolina Pawelczyk
karolinapawelczyk.com
@karolina_pawelczyk_illu

pp. 132-141
Kelly Smith
birdyandme.com
@birdyandme

pp. 142-147
Lena Ker
lenaker.art
@lenaker

pp. 148-153
Lydia Bourhill
bourhillustration.com
@bourhillustration

pp. 154-165
Mila Gislon
milagislon.com
@mila_jeanette

pp. 166-177
Miyuki Ohashi
miyukiohashi.net
@miyuki_ohashi

pp. 178-187
Nicole Jarecz
nicole-jarecz.com
@nicolejareczillustration

pp. 188-201
Nina Cosford
ninacosford.com
@ninacosford

pp. 202-211
Posuka Demizu
posuka.net
@demizuposuka

pp. 212-219
Shay Ben Izhack
shaybenizhack.com
@shaybenizhack

pp. 220-231
Steve Quiles
steveq212designs.com
@steveq212nyc

pp. 232-239
Tanya Chulkova
tanyachulkova.com
@tanyachulkova

pp. 240-253
Viola Li
violali.com
@byviolali

© CHANEL for all CHANEL creations

Gabrielle Chanel quotes:

'To remain irreplaceable we must always be different' (p. 55)
    The Sumter Daily Item, 25 July 1957
'A woman who uses no perfume has no future' (p. 59)
    Leymarie, J. (1987). *Chanel*, Genève: Skira
'Always to take off, never to add' (p. 113)
    Time (New York), 22 August 1960
'It was my good fortune to realise early that simplicity is elegance' (p. 151)
    The Family, 14 October 1963
'Eccentricity was dying out. I hope, what's more, that I helped kill it off' (p. 201)
    Morand, P. (2008). *The Allure of Chanel*, London: Pushkin Press

Concept: Carolijn Domensino
Text: Siska Lyssens
Editing: Heather Sills
Book design: Tina De Souter

Sign up for our newsletter with news about new and forthcoming publications
on art, interior design, food & travel, photography and fashion as well as
exclusive offers and events. If you have any questions or comments about
the material in this book, please do not hesitate to contact our editorial team:
art@lannoo.com

© Lannoo Publishers, Belgium, 2025
THEMA: AKLB, AKT
D/2025/45/290
ISBN: 978-90-209-8868-0
www.lannoopublishers.com